My Sunday Best

The Telegraph

My Sunday Best

101 Curious Contemplations on Modern Life

OLIVER PRITCHETT

with cartoons by **MATT**

Aurum
Press

First published in Great Britain
2014 by Aurum Press Ltd
74—77 White Lion Street
Islington
London N1 9PF
www.aurumpress.co.uk

A catalogue record for this book is available from the British Library.

ISBN 978 1 78131 405 0

1 3 5 7 9 10 8 6 4 2
2014 2016 2018 2017 2015

Typeset in Berling by carrdesignstudio.con
Printed by CPI Group (UK) Ltd, Croydon, CR0 4YY

Contents

Introduction

Well, this is a nice surprise. It's very good of you to take the time to read this Introduction. Normally people like to skip this bit and plunge straight into the book, often deciding they might as well start at page 39 where things will really have got going.

I know there are some who like to put off the business of getting into a book, like delaying the pleasure of a good meal by rearranging the cutlery or very slowly unfolding the napkin. These readers stroke the cover, then read the flyleaf and the Index, go through the Acknowledgments, then really tackle that difficult page which mentions the copyright, gives the ISBN number, names the typesetter and salutes the printer. In the good old days they could also exercise their brains deciphering the year of publication, which was always given in Roman numerals. Anyway, I'd like to welcome them to this Introduction and thank them for their hard work so far.

To be honest, I am not entirely thrilled to have an Introduction. I think I would really prefer a Foreword.

The word 'Foreword' has gravitas. It would lend much-needed authority and dignity both to me and to this collection. A Preface would also be good. I am even secretly attracted to the idea of a Prologue, but I guess this would be considered pretentious.

For those of you who are still with me, I ought, without further ado (as they say), make the formal introductions. Reader, allow me to present The Book. This is a selection mostly of short columns I have written over the past few years for the 'Life' section of the *Sunday Telegraph*. For a bit of variety, I have also included some slightly longer, earlier pieces which appeared in both the *Sunday Telegraph* and the *Daily Telegraph*. I have been writing these for more than thirty-five years; many of the cuttings have been lost or turned crisp and yellow in neglected folders, but these few I have included are chosen because I rather liked them and they haven't dated too badly. Most importantly, I am hoping you will find them funny.

I have been a journalist for more than fifty years and most of those have been spent on the *Telegraph*. I was well into my career before I realised that I wasn't cut out for journalism. I am not good on the telephone, I don't like marching up to strangers and asking them impertinent questions, I'm not really interested in cultivating important people and, above all, I haven't got much time for facts. I would much rather speculate or make things up, let my imagination loose on subjects or claim some expertise which I don't actually possess. I certainly wouldn't claim to be offering a higher truth, but perhaps it is an alternative truth. The aim is simply to make readers smile, or even laugh. I am extremely grateful to all the *Telegraph* editors, assistant editors, features editors, comment editors, section editors and (especially) sub-editors who have indulged me in this over the years.

There is one thing I ought to explain. This collection contains four pieces about Good King Wenceslas and this is because, many Decembers ago, I challenged myself to write a different piece every year on the theme of this Christmas carol. A number of *Telegraph* readers caught on to this and told me they came to look forward to it as Christmas approached, so I realised I couldn't stop even if I wanted to. A nun from a convent in Surrey wrote to tell me that my Wenceslas piece had been read aloud to the sisters over breakfast, and after that she would write and tell me if the latest one was as good as last year's. She was a severe critic and kept me on my toes.

I don't know how I come up with other subjects. Mostly by pacing about and muttering to myself. At my age, it's not surprising that I am aware of a good many annoyances in modern life. I am very fortunate that 'Life' gives me a chance to make jokes about these things, which I hope stops me turning into too much of a grumpy old codger.

And so we come to Matt, who, of course, needs no Introduction. It is a total joy for me to have my son, the renowned *Telegraph* cartoonist, as a colleague. We have become a small family business. He has been illustrating my columns for years and years and there is a sort of game we play together. We have never spoken about it, but we have just somehow adopted the rule that I never tell him what my chosen subject is for the week and, when he gets my copy, he never tells me what he is going to draw. Sometimes I finish a piece and I think: 'This one is impossible. There is nothing visual he will be able to latch on to in this one; he will never come up with an illustration.' But, of course, he always does and I discover that he has dreamed up some brilliantly original variation on my theme, embellished my joke and produced another great drawing. That is why, oddly, I can open the *Sunday Telegraph* every week, turn to my column and know that I am going to get a lovely surprise.

The Time of Our Life

And on the Thirteenth Day of Christmas . . . I Snapped

As a result of global warming there is a severe shortage of pear trees and partridges this year and the bird flu scare has caused all French hens to be withdrawn from circulation. So here is a revised version of an old Christmas favourite.

All together now:

On the **First** day of Christmas my true love texted me:
A grovelling apologee

On the **Second** day of Christmas my true love sent to me:
Two shower gels,

And a grovelling apologee

On the **Third** day of Christmas my true love sent to me:
Three light ales,
Two shower gels, and a grovelling apologee

On the **Fourth** day of Christmas my true love sent to me:
Four potted plants,
Three light ales, two shower gels, and a grovelling
    apologee

On the **Fifth** day of Christmas my true love sent my
    mobile:
Five ghastly ringtones,
Four potted plants, three light ales, two shower
    gels etc.

On the **Sixth** day of Christmas my true love sent to me:
Six daffs a-wilting,
Five ghastly ringtones, four potted plants, three light
    ales etc.

On the **Seventh** day of Christmas my true love FedExed
    me:
Seven Bries a-stinking,
Six daffs a-wilting, five ghastly ringtones, four potted
    plants etc.

On the **Eighth** day of Christmas my true love sent my
PC:
Eight poems downloaded,
Seven Bries a-stinking, six daffs a-wilting, five ghastly
ringtones etc.

On the **Ninth** day of Christmas my true love sent to me:
Nine scented candles,
Eight poems downloaded, seven Bries a-stinking, six
daffs a-wilting etc.

On the **Tenth** day of Christmas my true love sent to me:
Ten jokey emails,
Nine scented candles, eight poems downloaded, seven
Bries a-stinking etc.

On the **Eleventh** day of Christmas my true love sent to
me:
Eleven panettones,
Ten jokey emails, nine scented candles, eight poems
downloaded etc.

On the **Twelfth** day of Christmas the bastard sent to me:
Twelve drying-up cloths,
Eleven panettones, ten jokey emails, nine scented
candles, eight poems downloaded, seven Bries

a-stinking, six daffs a-wilting, five ghastly ringtones,
four potted plants, three light ales, two shower gels
and a grovelling apologee

(On the **Thirteenth** day of Christmas the postman left
for me:
A note saying he had tried to deliver a package but I
was out.)

Bargains

Here is my cut-out-and-keep Bargain Hunter's
Calendar for 2012 (£2 off, if you buy it before
3 February).

January: January sales. Huge reductions on carpets and a
four-seater leatherette sofa for the price of a three-seater.
Thirty per cent off panettones. Clementine prices slashed.
A box of liqueur chocolates for next to nothing.

February: January sales extended by six weeks. Fantastic
bargains in gardening items, including 'everything must

go' sale at Gazebos Galore. Buy three lawn sprinklers and get a free sun lounger. On Valentine's Day, why not say 'I love you' with a half-price panettone?

March: Mad March prices for carpets. Get a free clementine with every square metre of Axminster.

April: Incredible Royal Wedding Anniversary sale on 29 April. Tiaras at silly prices. Buy a panettone and get a chance to win a horse-drawn carriage like William and Kate's.

May: Fifty per cent off 2012 calendars and diaries. Massive clear-out of Valentine cards. Three leaf blowers for the price of two.

June: Grab a two-seater sofa for the price of an armchair. First one hundred customers get free exciting celebrity chef recipe book, *Twenty Things to Do with a Stale Panettone.*

July: Record-breaking Olympics sale. Sprint, like Usain Bolt, to your nearest warehouse and pick up a fridge-freezer like a gold medal weightlifter. Nothing to pay until the 2016 Olympic Games in Rio.

August: Ski-equipment prices going rapidly downhill. Install gas central heating on the morning of 9 August and pay no VAT. Hurry! Stupendous carpet sale MUST end in March 2025.

September: Still a few gazebos left at rock-bottom prices.

October: Prices on DVD box sets falling like autumn leaves. Fridge-freezer prices crashing.

November: Avoid the Christmas rush and take advantage of amazing introductory offers on panettones. Time to splash out on a paddling pool – 20 per cent off, plus free duck.

December: 2013 January sales start on 4 December.

Arrangements

So, that's all sorted now. You're coming to us on Christmas Day because it's our turn, but you won't arrive until about 9 p.m. because you've promised to go to your cousins in Edinburgh for traditional nibbles and you're picking up your vegetarian daughter arriving at Heathrow from Calcutta. Of course you can bring your new Bulgarian friend; it will be lovely to meet him. The Wilkinsons' spaniel is also coming; it should have been the Wilkinsons, but they're going skiing and leaving the dog.

On Christmas morning we'll drive to the big car park in Nuneaton to hand over our cat to the Dangerfields (because it doesn't get on with the Wilkinsons' dog) and we've promised to stay and have a mince pie. We won't get out of the car but we'll wear paper hats.

On Christmas Eve, we will be exchanging presents with Margaret's side of the family and having a casserole. We'll stay for breakfast with them on the actual day but it will have to be at 6 a.m. because we have to get back for our traditional Christmas breakfast with the Gladstones. My side of the family will drop in sometime between 11 a.m. and 4.30 p.m. (I have to remember to get the TV people in to make the conversion because my brother

insists on watching the Queen in high definition). We'll have presents and a smallish turkey then, so we can rush a slice to Aunt June who is stuck at home with her hip and we'll pull a cracker with her. Then the main meal (plus vegetarian option and nut allergy precautions) will be at about midnight with luck.

On Boxing Day we'll drive over to Tim and Jenny who put off their 'proper' Christmas for us, so we can't let them down – having first dropped off your daughter with her friends in Exeter. Simple really.

Cupid

How will Cupid be spending Valentine's Day this Thursday? 'I'll probably get up quite late, then toddle down to the archery club at midday, catch up with some mates and then maybe go somewhere for a few drinks,' the Roman god of love told me in an exclusive interview in his modest bedsit in Nottingham last week.

He now describes himself as 'semi-retired', a victim of the advance of internet dating, newspaper lonely hearts columns and, of course, health and safety. 'Nobody wants the personal touch any more,' he said, twanging his bowstring wistfully. 'The lads in the archery club have

seen pictures of me, in my loincloth and little wings and my curls, hovering above the ground, and they tease me about it. Luckily I have a gsoh.'

He still keeps in touch with 'the love business', as he calls it. 'I read the small ads. All those people claiming they like country walks and going to the theatre. The hillsides must be crawling with vivacious petite spinsters bumping into fit retired professionals. And you can't get a seat in the theatre because they've all been taken by down-to-earth cultured singles.'

Cupid can sometimes be spotted – well wrapped up these days in an old tweed overcoat and a woolly hat – standing between the lines of traffic heading into Nottingham, selling those bunches of roses which never get to flower.

'I've got some business ideas on the go,' he said. 'I'd like to take advantage of the modern technology. I'm trying to develop a Cupid app; it would be some kind of bow and arrow game probably. Or it could be an app that gives you all the words that rhyme with "blue". You know, to go with the roses-are-red-violets-are-blue sort of thing.'

I asked him if he had ever thought of getting hooked up with a partner. 'I once tried speed-dating,' he sighed. 'It wasn't really me.'

Father's Day

Only one week to go until Father's Day, so here are some last-minute present suggestions:

A 'Best Dad in the World' chequebook cover and pen. This is a present that keeps on giving. Every time he has to write you a cheque he will feel a warm parental glow.

Activity presents are increasingly popular for Father's Day, so have you considered a bungee-jumping treat for Dad? Or there's indoor rock climbing, snorkelling in particularly cold water, or hang-gliding. Here's something he will really appreciate: a beautifully forged framed certificate stating that on this Father's Day he did a free-fall

parachute jump. The date can be changed for subsequent Father's Days, so he can have a great sense of achievement without any of the risk.

Or get him the handsome leather-bound book with blank pages of handmade paper. On the cover, in gold lettering, it says, 'Things I Was Right About All Along'. The book has a padlock and key so your father can keep its contents secret.

Personalised presents are all the rage. This time, get him something else besides personalised cufflinks. (He already has fourteen pairs and all his shirts have buttoned cuffs.) It's now possible to buy attractively packaged person-alised Brillo pads, or earplugs or corn plasters.

He is bound to appreciate a rubber 'Severe Face' mask which he can wear when he wants to put his foot down. (This follows last year's hugely successful 'I'm Listening' mask.)

It's now possible to get wallpaper covered with the hand and foot prints of your new baby. Surprise a new dad by using it to redecorate his study.

Newspaper compilations of all the terrible things that happened in any specific year, going back to 1940, are now available. They come in a book called 'It Was Worse in My Day'. Lavishly illustrated with grim black-and-white photographs. Your dad will love it.

A Halloween Ghost Story

Joanna, a fitness instructor, and her husband Clive, a successful garden designer, moved into their new barn conversion in the autumn, just when the Gloucestershire countryside was looking its loveliest. The estate agents had described the property as 'charmingly haunted' and that had attracted them almost as much as the exposed beams.

'It will be a good way of getting to know the locals when the children come round for trick or treat,' Joanna said. 'I've bought the organic pumpkin and I've got in a good supply of Fairtrade dark chocolate.'

'And I've got a set of Sabatier knives specially designed for carving pumpkins,' said Clive. He hollowed out the pumpkin, gave it a face which was frightening, yet non-threatening, and put a hand-poured candle inside, with a burn time of twelve hours.

Nobody came; children hurried past their house; the chocolate was uneaten. They slept fitfully that night. Eerie sighing came from the kitchen, the cutlery drawer rattled, the Aga shuddered and they nearly jumped out of their duvet at the clanging of their copper sauté pan from Divertimenti.

Next morning, an appalling sight met their eyes when they went into the kitchen. The pumpkin was shredded,

17

the candle had dripped over their pine-topped work surface and there on the Aga (oh horror!) was a pumpkin risotto. Joanna screamed and was sick on her trainers.

Later, the oldest arboriculturist in the village came to espalier-train their pear trees and he told them a disturbing story. 'They do say a TV chef lived here once,' he said. 'Seems he disgraced himself when his autumn squash and walnut soup tragically curdled live on camera and he ended his days delivering pizzas. Folks believe his restless soul still wanders in converted kitchens.'

Joanna and Clive have now put the property on the market. The advertisement says: 'In need of some exorcism.'

Leap Year

I sense there is less enthusiasm for Leap Year these days. Women no longer need the support of a bit of dodgy folklore to justify proposing marriage to a man, if they feel like it. Maybe they could use 29 February for other proposals – that he gets rid of that hideous sweater, gives up wearing jeans or stops saying 'no prob' all the time.

The point is that proposing marriage was once considered strictly the man's department, so, in revising the folklore, we need to think of existing male domains that may be invaded by women once every four years. Wielding the power drill is not it; that territory has already been surrendered. We must think of something a woman could do that would make a man twitch with anxiety. Let's say that in a Leap Year a woman is allowed to choose a man's new car. Not bad, but not quite good enough.

Things a man considers his speciality are usually connected with burning. He believes that he is the only person in the household who can light a fire; he has his special way of constructing it in the grate. Once it is lit, he returns every twenty minutes to see how it is getting on and to reassure himself that he has done a marvellous job. And there's also the old cliché about men and barbecues.

At last I believe I have invented the perfect piece of folklore for the occasion. We can even say it goes back hundreds of years. The rule is that, in a Leap Year, women are in charge of all bonfires for the whole twelve months. Men are not allowed to go near; they must stay in the house and watch wistfully through the window. Meanwhile the woman of the house can stand beside her very own bonfire, arms folded proprietorially, watching it dreamily for hours.

Manual

Many of you will be getting electronic gadgets as presents this Christmas and these will come with an instruction manual. Correct use of this booklet is essential and, as a service to *Telegraph* readers, I have produced this exclusive *User Guide to the Instruction Manual*.

1. First, some important safety notes. You will observe that your manual is oblong and has four sharp corners (see fig. 2b). Do NOT jab any of these into your eye, as this can cause pain. Do not plug your manual into the mains or read it under water. Do NOT hold it over a naked flame.

2. Preparing the manual for use. Remove it from its wrapper and lay it on a flat, dry surface where there is adequate lighting. If your eyesight is deficient, put on spectacles and make sure they are securely in place. You will notice that your manual is fitted with two staples (see fig. 14c). Do NOT remove the staples as this will cause the pages to separate.

3. In order to maximise the benefit and pleasure you derive from your manual you should read it in the language in which you are most fluent. Do NOT attempt to follow the operating instructions in Korean unless Korean is your first language. There is usually a choice of six languages in your manual (except in the KG906-211X where there are nine). Make sure you know which is your first language BEFORE attempting to read the manual.

4. It is advisable to have a ten-year-old child handy when reading the operating instructions.

5. On the last page of the manual you will find the telephone number of a Helpdesk. DELETE this as it is irrelevant and will only cause confusion.

6. Troubleshooting. If you get stuck and 'freeze' when you reach page four, place the manual in the kitchen drawer (with all the others) and leave it there for at least six months.

May Day

I have solved the mystery of all those ancient May Day customs, such as dancing round the maypole, crowning the May Queen and skipping about waving branches of apple blossom. These were, in fact, clever excuses for getting out of all the do-it-yourself jobs – which were an even more ancient tradition associated with the first weekend in May.

In the Middle Ages, when a man was told by his wife that the wattle and daub of his rude dwelling could do with re-daubing, he had the perfect get-out. He could explain that unfortunately he was going to be tied up at the maypole all day.

This is undoubtedly how Morris dancing evolved. On May Day in Tudor times when a man was supposed to be weatherproofing his Tudor beams ('It doth exactly what it saith on the tinne') he could say the job was absolutely top of his list of things to do, but he was committed to meeting some other chaps to perform this wretched fertility rite. Terrible nuisance, but it had to be done – otherwise there would be no fertility.

You will notice that Morris dancing, like most May Day customs, is a mainly male occupation. Historically (but not so much these days) May Day DIY has been a male chore. QED.

I'm not one of those who mock Morris dancers; I admire their ingenuity. If you want your Tudor beams to be weatherproofed or your bathroom tiles to be grouted or your wattle and daub knocked through, the last person you are going to ask is a man who skips about with bells on his knees while flapping a hankie. That is the perfect way of conveying the message: 'I'm absolutely hopeless at those practical things.'

So, today I will leave that new tin of non-drip gloss unopened while I go off and look for a May Queen to crown.

Mother's Day

Today this column is teaming up with a number of businesses to offer some truly stunning Mother's Day treats. For a start, here's a new twist on the old breakfast in bed tradition: Stan's Speedy Removals will carry off the bed (with Mum in it, of course) and plonk it down on the beauty spot of your choice, such as the White Cliffs of Dover, so she can admire some stunning views while enjoying her lightly boiled egg. She also gets a complimentary glass of Prosecco.

Or perhaps she'd enjoy a bit of pampering a few hundred feet up in the air. The Dinkie Pinkie Nail Bar will give her a pedicure in a hot-air balloon – with chocolates, string quartet and Prosecco thrown in, *naturellement*.

Ever wanted to make your mother queen for a day? Here's your opportunity: give her the chance to lay a foundation stone. G&S Builders' Merchants are offering this treat to anyone buying two bags of cement. There will be a top etiquette expert on hand to teach her the art of the royal wave, and she also gets a DVD recording of the event to treasure for ever.

Here are some other unrepeatable offers. If you call out Whizzee Klene emergency drain-unblocking service today, their team of drain engineers will serenade your mother with her favourite songs in close harmony; and if you go to any branch of Joe's Beefy Burger Bar chain for a traditional Sunday lunch, mother gets a free portion of heart-shaped deep-fried onion rings – and, you guessed it, a complimentary glass of Prosecco.

Finally, a once-in-a-lifetime experience: thanks to Worksop & Bolsover Accident Insurance Co, it's mums-go-free day on the Cresta Run. And when they have finished hurtling at 80mph, they can raise a glass of Prosecco to toast the fact that Mother's Day is one institution that has never succumbed to commercialisation.

Presents

It is time for my annual list of Clever Christmas Present Ideas:

1. A Skip

Imagine the delight on the faces of your friends as they wake up on Christmas Day to find a skip parked outside their house. It will be perfect for dumping all the cardboard, bubble wrap and polystyrene packaging that accumulates over the festive season, and also a wonderful opportunity to get round to that house clear-out they've been putting off for years.

When they have filled their skip with their junk you can have it taken away and parked outside the house of someone who has a birthday in January. They will thank you for the happy hours they spend rummaging through it.

2. A Candle De-scenter

At Christmas our senses are assailed by the sickly smell of scented candles. This clever device removes all those tiresome pongs of gardenia and lily of the valley. Your friends just have to place their candles inside the de-scenter for an hour. Then, when the inevitable power cuts occur, they will have odour-free candlelight.

3. 'Soap on a Hope'

With this imaginative charity, presents of soap and bath salts, which you would have given to your aunt, are sent to a Third World country instead. Your aunt gets a certificate and a nice warm feeling.

4. A Doctor's Note

Handwritten on finest parchment and in an ornate silver gilt frame, this note excuses the recipient from free-fall parachuting, white-water rafting, rides down the Cresta Run and any other alarming experience some other person may have given them for Christmas.

5. Adopt-a-Poinsettia

When someone is given a plant they also get all the worry of its upkeep. Your friends will be so relieved to know that their poinsettia is in good hands, at the florists, who will send them a photo and regular updates on how it is getting on. (Also available in amaryllis.)

Sleigh

IMPORTANT. Please read these Safety Notes before taking part in the One Horse Open Sleigh Experience.

1. We encourage responsible jingling on our sleigh rides and, for that reason, it will not be possible for passengers to 'jingle all the way'. When the orange light shows, this indicates a quiet period, as o'er the fields we go, and you should refrain from all jingling. This is to ensure that prolonged noise does not get on the horse's nerves and cause it to behave erratically.

2. For the same reason, laughing all the way is discouraged.

3. Wassailers and any gentlemen deemed to be merry, in the judgment of the on-sleigh safety officer, will not be permitted on the ride. No beverages may be taken on board.

4. Please wear your high-visibility jacket at all times. This will enable our pick-up team to locate you in the snowdrifts in the unlikely event that you are thrown out of the sleigh – which, as stated in the terms and conditions, is open – i.e. has no roof. Those who have chosen the 'dashing through the snow' experience (no children allowed) will also be required to wear safety belts.

5. Please observe the signs warning of low overhead branches and duck when requested.

6. Reindeer can be unpredictable, so, in the event that your one-horse open sleigh encounters another sleigh, piled with presents and driven by a bearded man, certain precautionary measures will have to be taken. Passengers will adopt the 'crouch' position and all jingling will cease until the safety officer gives the all clear.

7. If you have any queries about any safety aspects of your ride, please contact the team at *www.owhatfun.com* and we will be happy to deal with your concerns.

Finally, the O What Fun Festive Leisure Corporation and its affiliates accept no responsibility for any hats which may get blown off in the course of the ride.

Sprouts

Some unfortunate members of society will be now living in dread. This is because they have heard the news that the unusually warm winter weather this year has helped to create a bumper crop of Brussels sprouts. For some, a single green sphere of this vegetable can turn Christmas lunch into a living hell.

Fortunately, a lot of good work is being done to support sufferers from brassicaphobia – or sprout-haters – and get them accepted by society and help them lead a normal lunch. There are support groups all over the country where they can meet other sufferers and know they are not alone. They are encouraged to act out their fear of sprouts and to face up to past bad experiences with the vegetable. Psychologists say that a single sprout can somehow come to symbolise all bad Christmas memories.

One way to help is get the sufferer to 'adopt' a sprout. He or she is taken to a field when the vegetable is just a pimple on a stalk. With regular weekly visits, the patient learns to bond with it. Mentoring is also an important part of the treatment. Volunteers will be on call throughout Christmas Day to come and sit beside brassicaphobes at the dinner table and encourage them to stick a fork in the dreaded veg.

Scientists are also conducting trials of a drug that may cure a fear of sprouts, but, at the moment, they are encountering some distressing side-effects – such as a violent hostility to Christmas trees.

Often a dislike of sprouts may be due to an allergy to the EU and the association with Brussels. A solution may be found in 'Yorkshire sprouts', which are being marketed for the first time this year and advertised on TV with the slogan: 'There's nowt like a good, honest Yorkshire sprout. It's right delicious with a dollop of Yorkshire brandy butter.'

Sustainable Santa

Children will be thrilled to learn that Father Christmas is now fully sustainable. On behalf of 'Life' readers, I was granted an exclusive interview with Santa and I visited him in his hi-tech home designed by Scandinavia's foremost eco-architect Lars Thörsday. Special features of the house, close to the North Pole, include solar panels specially adapted for the midnight sun, a heating system using only recycled reindeer dung, and clever use of space for the storage of toys.

Mrs Christmas has a full-time consultancy specialising in green issues, so Father Christmas is very much the house-husband, supervising the work of the elves who are engaged in an exciting moss-conservation project. 'Living in this part of the world I am well aware that climate change is no ho-ho-ho matter,' Santa told me.

All letters sent by children are compacted into bricks to build the elves' quarters – after the children's requests have been copied onto the Clausmatron 3XDM computer. This year Father Christmas has the latest thing in sleighs – a super-lightweight aluminium number with aerodynamic features. Two fewer reindeers are needed to pull it, so these two now produce the milk for Santa's range of certified organic locally sourced artisan reindeer cheeses.

Father Christmas has managed to reduce reindeer miles by 17 per cent by changing his Christmas Eve course so that it passes the maximum number of wind farms to blow the sleigh along. 'Since October I've been working with my personal fitness elf, running eight miles a day carrying a sack of toys, so I'm in condition for the big day,' he said. He has also been watching his diet, to slim down for the chimneys.

'I'll let you into a secret,' he told me exclusively. 'I don't eat the mince pies the children leave out; I take them home for the elves. I just eat the raw carrots meant for the reindeer.'

Valentine

This week, as Valentine's Day approaches, I am combining my duties as health and fitness guru with my role as agony uncle. Here is a selection of questions from my postbag:

Q. *I am suffering from a broken heart. Will this affect my overall fitness?*

A. Actually a broken heart is potentially a great aid to wellbeing. A programme of heavy sighing can do wonders for your lung capacity and will also tone up those stomach muscles. Try to begin your day with thirty heart-rending sighs. Follow this with some heaving sobs when you have your mid-morning energy drink. Sighing and sobbing are an excellent form of exercise, as they can be done anywhere, including at your office desk. Tear ducts also benefit from regular weeping, but be sure to dispose of those soggy hankies responsibly.

Q. *I have been pursuing this man for several months. He is my personal trainer and I've been trying to catch up with him on our morning run to tell him I love him. But I am doubled-up and so breathless I can't get the words out.*

A. Try fainting to attract his attention. Many men find that attractive in a woman. But first, check that he is a qualified first-aider.

Q. *Last Valentine's Day, my boyfriend took me out for a romantic dinner and the oysters made me vomit over his dozen red roses. How can I avoid this happening again?*

A. Tell him to skip the oysters and remind him of the aphrodisiac qualities of a cauliflower smoothie.

Q. *I am in love with the receptionist at my GP's practice. I go there frequently with minor complaints just to see her. When I ask her out on a date, she is cold, negative and unhelpful. How can I win her?*

A. Contact your doctor directly and ask him (or her) to make an appointment for you to see the receptionist. That's your only chance.

Flip-flops

Today has been designated the official start of the flip-flop season. This is the time of the year when large numbers of people in British towns and cities try to deceive their feet into thinking they are in some charming little-known Mediterranean port or strolling back from the beach in St Tropez. Come to think of it, you don't really stroll in flip-flops; you slop.

By the way, I am the one doing the designating; I just thought flip-flops should have a season with a definite start date, like grouse shooting. I know some people have slipped into their flip-flops long before today, but they should be told they have committed a grave social *faux pas*. Actually, 'flip-flop' is not really the noise made by people walking along in this particular type of footwear. It's more of a kind of squelch, so that when somebody approaches you from behind in the street you feel you are being followed by a giant snail travelling at speed.

Sometimes, as the sole of the foot parts company with the base of the flip-flop, it sounds like masking tape being ripped off a pane of glass, then at other times the effect is more of a live fish flapping about on linoleum. When somebody is unwise enough to run in flip-flops they go flippity-floppity splat. And when they are caught in a sudden shower of rain they go slurp-slop.

As summer wears on and I feel I am being assailed by slurps and squelches I begin to yearn for the serene autumn silence of trainers and Ugg boots or even the crisp rat-a-tat-tat of stilettoes on the pavement. Then I tell myself to be grateful for the extraordinary variety of sounds that can be made by these simple objects reacting to the human foot. Somebody should combine them all and compose a symphony which would perfectly evoke our summer.

Pancakes

Pancake Day this year promises to be the best ever. Indeed it has been calculated that if all the pancakes made in Britain next Tuesday were put together into one giant pancake it would cover an area the size of the Isle of Wight. (Plans to actually cover the Isle of Wight with a giant pancake have been put on hold, because of the cost at this time of economic difficulty.)

Britain is among the world leaders in the making of pancakes, both the ready-mix and made-from-scratch varieties. Professor Ian Lumpish, Head of Batter Studies at the University of Thirsk, says this is due to our heritage of fish and chips and toad-in-the-hole. 'Quite literally, we have batter in our blood,' he says.

To help you fully enjoy Pancake Day it's important to observe a few safety rules. These can be found in the new government leaflet, *Have a Flipping Great Day*. In the chapter entitled 'Don't Take a Risk with That Whisk!' you will see that all electric whisks must now be inspected annually by a certified electrical appliance safety officer. And if you whisk by hand there are diagrams showing the correct grip and recommended clockwise motion to be used to avoid wrist sprain. There is also a timely warning about the link between excessive pancake consumption and obesity.

Tossing pancakes above a certain height is now banned for safety reasons. The maximum pan-to-air toss is set at 24cm. However, some local councils have teams of qualified tossers (wearing high-visibility jackets and carrying official identify cards) who will come to your house and flip your pancakes for you.

Mr Cameron is expected to lend his wholehearted support to Britain's pancake makers on Tuesday and to send out an optimistic message about the role of batter in leading our economic recovery. His theme will be: 'Today, the pancake; tomorrow, the waffle.

A Hard Life

Wenceslas

Hi, am I speaking to Mr Peasant? Oh great, very merry Feast of Stephen to you, Mr Peasant. How are you this evening? That's brilliant. Just a quick call about your winter fuel needs, if I may. My name is Wenceslas, from the Outlook Team of the Good King Power Company plc. First of all, for security, can you give me the first line of your address? A good league hence? That's lovely, Mr Peasant. And could you tell me the name of the fountain in your postcode? That's great. So the full address is: a good league hence, underneath the mountain, right against the forest fence? That's wonderful.

Now, Yonder – you don't mind me calling you Yonder, I hope? That's superb. Anyway, it being a very bright moonlit night, I noticed you making your way across the deep and crisp and even snow picking up your winter fuel and I thought it would be a good time to talk about your tariff. Do you realise, that for a little extra, you could qualify for our pine logs option? Or, if you prefer, we could sign you up right away for our flesh and wine package.

You know only too well how cruel the frost can be, Yonder, so the beauty of the pine logs option (with or without the flesh and wine upgrade) is that you spread the payments over the whole year and you will never be without winter fuel. In an emergency, your local St Agnes Fountain rep, Mike Page, can get pine logs delivered to the door of your hovel within three hours. Even in dreadful weather like this, as he can drive his van along the route where the Good King Power Company plc dinting lorries have cleared a path.

While I've got you on the line, would you be interested in our insurance cover for home appliances and fountain leaks and accidental damage to forest fences? Hello, Mr Peasant, are you still there . . . ?

Wenceslas Wishes You Were Here . . .

Their Majesties King Wenceslas and Queen Berta are currently on holiday in Barbados and will not be back in Bohemia until early in the New Year. They take this opportunity to wish all their friends a very happy Christmas. Even though they are far away, their thoughts will be with their people, especially on the Feast of Stephen.

Instead of sending Christmas cards this year, King Wenceslas is making donations to a number of charities. A full list of these can be found on his website www. wenceslas.com/lookout (click on 'Good' and follow the links), but here are some of the main causes the King and Queen are supporting:

Hither and Yonder. This is the umbrella organisation for a number of self-help groups undertaking community projects in the St Agnes area. A great deal of work still needs to be done to restore the fine old St Agnes Fountain to its former glory after it was saved from the developers by an energetic local campaign. It is also hoped to build a community centre for peasant mothers and toddlers.

Money will also be used for essential repairs to the forest fence.

Give a Boar. Once again, King Wenceslas is supporting this admirable scheme started by Bohfam, to donate wild boars to the poorest inhabitants of the forest region to help them support themselves by raising livestock. There were teething problems with the scheme last year, but now the important stretch of the forest fence has been repaired and most of the victims of mauling have recovered from the worst of their injuries. Lessons have been learned and it is time to move ahead with this scheme.

The Campaign for a Sustainable Bohemia. Thanks to the wonderful work of the popular singer Krok, awareness has been raised of the problem of depleting stocks of pine logs. The only solution is to turn to some form of sustainable energy, and that is why it is so important to support the plans for a wind farm a good league hence from His Majesty's castle. More needs to be done to win over local objectors. Some dwellings will have to be demolished.

Deep and Crisp. This is the charity founded by that wonderful organisation Snow Concern and it is, of course, closely tied to Their Majesties' other environmental interests. Do you remember when the moon shone brightly, the frosts were cruel and the wind blew stronger? All that could disappear if we don't do something urgently about climate change. Pretty soon there could be no snow to lie dinted. Scientists say that, if nothing is done, by the year 989 flood water could reach the level of the turret of the castle from which King Wenceslas usually looks out on the Feast of Stephen.

Stand by Me. We all know about the growing problem of delinquency in the St Agnes area, having seen it with our own eyes. Many theories have been put forward to explain this. Some say it is boredom, because peasant youths don't have enough facilities, while others claim it is the result of being exposed to the constant violent spectacle of vicious wild boars rampaging and goring people.

King Wenceslas had personal experience of the problem when, last Feast of Stephen, a guest of his (a yonder peasant, as it happens) was mugged while making his way home from the castle, somewhat inebriated after a convivial night. In July Their Majesties held a charity ball in aid of Stand by Me.

Tread Thou Boldly. Queen Berta is patron of this charity, which runs a retirement home especially for former pages with frostbitten feet. Alas, inadequate footwear for manservants is a long-standing problem in Bohemia, and they are often expected to go out at all hours of day and night. Tread Thou Boldly offers them expert nursing care and treatment by the nation's top chiropodists. Before they left for Barbados, King Wenceslas and Queen Berta donated a substantial amount of flesh and wine for a charity auction to raise funds to buy a mini-sledge to take patients on outings round our beautiful forested region.

Wenceslas – the Truth

It has always seemed to me a rather suspicious coinci-dence. We are asked to believe that Good King Wenceslas just *happened* to look out at the precise moment that the poor man came in sight. It is all too convenient. If he had looked out a minute too soon he would have noticed nothing but snow.

And if he had left it two minutes longer, the poor man would have been out of sight, having already gathered enough winter fuel, and would be hurrying back home. Wenceslas would have summoned his page to stand by him, pointed to the disturbed area of snow and asked: 'Yonder footprints, whose are they?'

And the page would have said: 'Oh, it's probably that peasant who lives a good league hence, underneath the mountain. Perhaps he's been gathering winter fuel, or something.' Good King Wenceslas would have shrugged and sat down again.

My theory is that Wenceslas *kept* looking out on that particular Feast of Stephen. Every couple of minutes, he would go over to the aperture in the castle wall, look out and say something like: 'Brightly shines the moon tonight.' Then he would pace up and down a bit, whistle 'Jingle Bells' under his breath, kick one of the pine logs in the fireplace, go and look out again and say, to nobody in particular: 'The frost's cruel, though.'

The Queen would look up from her improving embroidery, frown and say: 'Oh, do stop fidgeting.'

The explanation for the behaviour of Wenceslas must be that he was expecting someone. He was carrying on in the way people do when they are waiting for guests to arrive.

After years of research among mouldering manuscripts and dank archives in eastern Europe, I have been able to establish that the Wenceslases were in the habit of holding 'Open Castle' on the Feast of Stephen. They would send out invitations to anybody who was anybody in tenth-century Bohemia, asking them to drop in at any time during the day for a flesh and wine buffet.

On this occasion, the whole day passed and nobody had arrived. Wenceslas kept looking out, then sidling to the table where the food was laid out. The Queen told him not to pick at it because someone might still arrive, even at this hour.

At first, he had not worried. 'With this snow lying all about,' he told the Queen and the page several times, 'it's bound to be a slow start. Things will soon pick up.' But his looking out became more and more frequent.

There were messages. The Wenceslases' dearest friends, Adrian and Molly, who only lived a few leagues hence as the crow flies, sent word. 'Don't know what it's like where you are,' they said, 'but it's deep and crisp and even hereabouts and we just don't think we could get through.'

Wenceslas sent a message back saying: 'I'm sure you will be all right if you drive your horse-drawn sleigh through the part of the track where the snow lies dinted.' But Adrian said he couldn't find anybody to help him jump-start his horse.

And the Duchess of Moravia, who was normally so game about showing up, sent a servant to say that she had been struck down by this ghastly bug which was going round. 'It's particularly nasty, this Bohemian flu,' the Queen observed. The duchess's servant complained that he had chilblains, so Wenceslas told him about the dinted-snow trick and sent him on his way.

The evening wore on and nobody came. 'It's all a bit of a frost,' said Wenceslas, looking out for the thousandth time. The page, who had been hired from an agency for the occasion, wondered when he would be allowed to knock off. 'I know not how I can go no longer,' he whispered to the cook.

'Shhh,' said the cook. 'I think I heard Wenceslas calling you thither.'

So the page found himself trudging through the snow, treading in his master's steps, to fetch yonder peasant to the party. The peasant had, in fact, been on his way to a bit of a do with friends right against the forest fence when he had been spotted by the king. 'Bring some kindling,' the invitation had said.

Out of politeness, he stayed and made conversation about the weather. 'Yes, it is deep where I live,' he said to the Queen. 'But maybe not as crisp and even as it is here.'

In my researches I found one fascinating document which was written a year after the events in the carol. It says: 'The Wenceslases are spending the Feast of Stephen abroad this year and take this opportunity to send good wishes to all their friends.'

Wenceslas Wants its Pound of Flesh

From: The Department of Rural Community Affairs, Lower Bohemia Region

Dear Yonder Peasant,

An audit of this department's accounts shows you were allocated an excess number of pine logs on the Feast of Stephen last year. This was due to a fault in our new Wenceslas computer system, which was installed to improve the efficiency of pine log distribution. The shining of very bright moonlight on the night in question damaged the software, leading to this error, which we regret. Please arrange to return the pine logs to this department by this coming Feast of Stephen.

Yours sincerely,
H. Page
(Assistant to Senior Welfare Officer,
Lower Bohemia Region)

Dear Mr Page,

Your letter has only just reached me because it was sent to the wrong address. My dwelling is right against the forest fence, by St Agnes Fountain, not, as you put on the envelope, by St Andrews Fountain, which is a good eight leagues hence. The other thing is, I have burned most of those logs, it being very cold. The snow is laying round about and it's deep, crisp and even. Not to mention the frost being cruel. In these conditions, it will be hard for me to make the journey to your department. Wouldn't it be possible for you to come hither, Mr Page?

Yours,
Y. Peasant

Dear Mr Peasant,

We are sorry we got your address wrong. Discs containing the details of many peasants sadly went astray some months ago and we are having to build up our database again from scratch. The Minister for Rural Community Affairs has apologised and taken steps to ensure it never happens again. Please let the authorities know if you think your data may have fallen into the wrong hands. We have no machinery for collecting excess pine logs. Please ensure they are returned in the next ten days.

H. Page

Dear Page,

Please find enclosed a small amount of ash from the pine logs I was sent last year. I will post further instalments soon but, knowing the postal service, it will be months before you receive them.

Yrs,

Peasant

Dear Peasant,

I am informed by our Looking Out Team that you have been in the habit of gathering winter fuel. For some reason, this information does not appear in the program of the new Wenceslas computer system. It means you never actually qualified for free pine logs but were eligible to receive a voucher for three bundles of kindling wood. To improve efficiency, these vouchers will no longer be distributed on the Feast of Stephen, but in mid-August.

H. Page

Dear Page,

What are you going to do about St Agnes Fountain, which has been out of action since last Feast of Stephen when the pipes burst? Three lots of your people have been round to look at it, but nothing has been done.

Y.P.

Dear Peasant,

It has come to light that, due to a glitch with the Wenceslas computer, you were also given flesh and wine you were not authorised to receive last year. Please return these with the pine logs.

H. Page

Look, Mr So-Called Assistant to the So-Called Senior Welfare Officer,

I ate the flesh and I drank the wine. That's what you're supposed to do. I might be able to return a rabbit bone with the one pine log I've been saving up, but I don't know how. Have you noticed that the nights grow darker now and the wind blows stronger?

Y. Peasant

Dear Mr Peasant,

I enclose a copy of our booklet called *How to Tread Where the Snow Lies Dinted*, which should help you with your journey. Please note that this office will be closed for the Feast of Stephen holiday, re-opening on 9 January. You may leave your pine logs at the back door of the Wenceslas Castle Leisure and Heritage Centre. On behalf of the department, I wish you a Merry Christmas.

Plant and Animal Life

Cyclamen

The pink cyclamen passed away peacefully last night. It was not unexpected. Since it was given to us just before Christmas, its health had been very much up and down. Like all cyclamen, it was a bit of a drama queen, drooping suddenly and tragically, then reviving unexpectedly. I had this theory that, in spite of their dainty appearance, cyclamen are not keen on central heating and prefer more rugged conditions. It certainly braced up after a night on the frosty balcony, but then went into a decline again.

Meanwhile the condition of the potted azalea is officially described as 'poorly' and the orchid-thing is as well as can be expected. The truth is, we are not fit people to look after potted plants. African violets arrive in our house and immediately get homesick, crocus bulbs cower in their pots and never show their heads above the surface. The fate of the amaryllis in 1983 is a dark family secret. Still, the potted plants arrive every December. You could say that we have measured out our Christmases with cyclamen corpses.

Taking on a plant should be like adopting a rescue dog; severe ladies should come round and check us out in advance, taking note of the draughts and the light, cross-questioning us for hours and finally telling us: 'We have decided with regret that you are not the sort of people who should be entrusted with bringing up a hyacinth.'

It's not all our fault. Those pointy plastic labels giving instructions on the care of the plant are hopelessly vague. 'Do not over-water,' they say. Thanks a lot. I lurch round the room several times a day, carrying the azalea and searching for 'moderate' sunlight. The labels are in several languages, so I know that the Dutch for 'keep moderately moist' is '*matig vochtig houden*'. We have dozens of them, left over from previous plant fatalities. I'm going to use them to teach myself Dutch.

Al Fresco

To me, the most doom-laden eight words of the summer are: 'I thought we'd have lunch in the garden.' Moments after the hostess or host has uttered them, we will all gather round the table and help shift it a couple of feet, to be a little more in the shade. Then I always choose the wrong place to sit, so I'm staring straight into the sun while the blur of the person opposite says, 'Isn't this lovely?'

'So relaxing,' I reply as my chair gives a terrible lurch. This is because we're on a patio of lovely rough-hewn rustic stone and everything wobbles. It's the charm of rustic stone. While blinded by the sun, I'm also disorientated by the continuous annoying trickle of the water feature somewhere nearby.

There's always one more thing to fetch from the kitchen – a spoon for the potato salad, the strawberries, another bottle of that interesting home-made elderflower cordial. I like to volunteer for these fetching duties; if I keep moving it means my bottom will be less corrugated by the garden chair. That's why I'm always first onto my feet to chase the paper napkins which blow away towards the bed of lupins.

Now it's time for us all to stand up again and shift the table a few more inches. It's more in the shade now, but rockier. There's something wrong with the design of garden furniture; something about the journey taken by the food from plate to mouth which makes it have to travel across a vast expanse of lap and shirt. I have an oily patch on my front, from the (highly praised) vinaigrette and a strawberry nestles on my left thigh, next to the piece of potato salad. Maybe nobody will notice if I keep moving. I surreptitiously release my napkin into the wind and make a dash in pursuit of it into the lupins.

Merchandise

Alan Titchmarsh was complaining the other day that we have lost many of our gardening skills because instant technology has left us 'afraid of the earth' or too impatient to wait for things to grow. I wonder if it may also be because we have become more interested in the merchandise than in the actual cultivation. We're enticed by the trugs, the elegantly floppy hats, the witty T-shirts, the scented soap for hand-washing afterwards, the ornate boot-scrapers, the quaint bird tables and the painted signs saying 'I'm Pottering in the Garden'.

All I have is a small London balcony with a bush, a frost-cracked tub and two defeated geraniums, but I long to have all these horticultural extras. Among the cascade of catalogues coming through my letterbox last week was one which offered all kinds of classy accessories, such as a cast-iron Victorian bird feeder (with faux rust finish) an Edwardian bird bath and various terracotta plaques. How I long to put up a sign saying 'I'm Lurking on the Balcony' and I dream of going out in designer wellies and floppy hat to sprinkle a little faux rust here and there. Maybe if I had bought (for £59.99) a frost-resistant faux lead statue of St Francis of Assisi he would have protected my tub.

So I just stand on the balcony and try to cheer up the geraniums. Maybe I should give up my gardening ambitions and dream up some ideas for accessories that I could market – things with a bit of an historical angle. I'm thinking of Tudor-style faux moss, to give your walls a bit of character, or medieval hawking gauntlets for use as gardening gloves, or a replica of King Arthur's round bird table. Then perhaps I could also produce a handsome leather-bound volume called *The Capability Brown Joke Book*, which would give details of his fifty best ha-has.

Garden Tips

Here are my tips on What to Do in Your Garden in April:

Check your patio furniture and replace the wedges of cardboard or old seed catalogues propping up the legs of chairs and tables on the uneven surface. Find a moment to go and practise unfolding the sun-lounger in private. Give your shed a good kick to see how far the rot has progressed. Look up the word 'perennial' in the dictionary. Shake the mouse droppings out of your wellington boots.

It's time to pay more attention to those seeds which you sowed in pots on the window ledge in late February and which you have been checking once a day for signs of life. From now on, you should be checking on them twice a day in preparation for giving up on them in the first week of May.

Spend some time cultivating your next-door neighbours who you have been neglecting through the winter months; you are going to have to borrow their lawnmower soon. It may be necessary to give them a good feed. Disentangle the hose. Use stakes to prop up things that need support – like the trellis.

Now is the time to improve the quality of soil in your borders. Give them a good sprinkling of all-purpose well-rotted garden shed. I also like to shake our doormat over them, as the old house dust, animal hairs and biscuit crumbs provide all the necessary nutrients.

Plant your early potatoes; remember it is essential to put them in before 8 a.m. Mids can be planted in mid-morning. By now you should have lost half a stone since Christmas. This is particularly important if you plan to grow early peas, which, of course, have to be sown thinly. Before you sow anything, make sure that the soil has warmed up sufficiently. It's a good idea to go over it first with a hairdryer or a blowtorch.

Leaf Blowers

The beauty of leaf blowers is that they can annoy other people in so many different ways. Obviously, the basic function is to create a noise which drives your neighbours mad from late September onwards, at a time when it is no longer practical to irritate them with barbecues and lawnmowers. While it takes about twenty-five minutes to rake the leaves off the average lawn, a leaf blower can move them about a bit for periods as long as an hour and a quarter.

Suppose you live at number 12 Dyspepsia Avenue and you realise that the chap along the road at number 44 is having a bonfire. It's enormous fun to herd your leaves all the way down the road to his bonfire, if necessary blowing them through his house. As you make your way down the street, other owners of leaf blowers will join in. And if, on the way, you pass any wet dogs returning from a walk, why not give them a quick blow-dry while you're about it?

When you finally get about a tenth of the leaves to the garden at number 44, you can all aim your leaf blowers at the bonfire to perk it up.

There's no need to put away your machine in the summer. If it's a sunny day and people are lounging in nearby gardens, bring out a couple of leaf blowers and have a game of blow badminton, sending the shuttlecock over the net with well-aimed blasts.

A wasp in the kitchen? Simple, just chase it away with the trusty leaf blower. Children have left pieces of Lego all over the house? All you do is blow them all into a heap and steer that heap into the children's bedroom. Works like magic. Gets the job done in three hours flat.

Next week: some tips on how to get the best out of revving your motorbike.

Open Gardens

We are now in the season when kind people open their gardens to the public. I'm talking about neighbours, not National Trust people or the gracious local gentry. It has always struck me that this is really just a form of licensed snooping. As merely the owner of a balcony with a few tubs on it, I've always felt uneasy on these occasions.

I'm hardly qualified to pass comment on somebody's rhododendrons and, anyway, I don't have the Latin. I'm also afraid I might compliment the green-fingered owner on a particularly striking weed. I'm reduced to comments like: 'Ooh, nice red ones, a bit bigger than the yellow ones', or 'Look, there's a wasp.' I stand in awe before the compost heap and I find I'm enchanted by a single daisy in the lawn. After this, I feel I hardly deserve the free tea and biscuits or the half-glass of white wine.

All the time, I'm trying to avert my eyes from the house, to resist the temptation to peer in through the window and check out the sitting room furnishings or linger by the open back door to smell what's cooking for dinner. What if I were to ask if I could use their loo? I bet this is one of the worst crimes in the book of garden visitors' etiquette – only slightly less heinous than being caught with a pair of secateurs concealed about your person. Actually, an etiquette guide would be really useful – plus a botanical phrase book.

In our bit of north London they also have open days for local artists' studios. Here's another minefield. It's just as hard to think of something to say about someone's gallant attempt at a still life as it is to think of the *mot juste* for some patiently cultivated shrub. I usually stand by the window in the artist's studio, staring out at the garden.

Seeds

Even with just two sad tubs on the balcony, I'm a keen vicarious gardener. This means I never get my hands and knees muddy. I adore seed catalogues for the sheer pleasure of all that Latin. All those lovely evocative words, like *elegans*, *giganteum*, *grandiflora*, *fragrantissima*, *variabilis* and *millefolium*. I was idly flicking through a catalogue the other day, now that spring is here, and I was delighted to come across the charming *Primula vulgaris*. It sounds like someone passing a snobbish remark about that processed cheese which comes in tubes. 'They're frightfully *Primula vulgaris*. Have you seen what she puts in her children's packed lunch?'

I also love the surprise when a good old English name is plonked at the end of a string of Latin words – as in *Lathyrus odoratus grandiflorus Miss Willmott*. This is described as a hardy annual climber and I'm sure that is no reflection on Miss Willmott's social ambitions.

And I was very struck by *Petunia grandiflora* 'Prism Pale Burgundy Vein' F1 Hybrid, which might easily be the official kennel name of some unexpectedly small and yappy dog at Crufts. In fact, it turns out to be an easy-going sort of flower which is quite happy in baskets, beddings, borders, containers, patios and tubs.

Of course there is always the suspicion that somebody showing you round their garden and using a lot of Latin is just putting on dog, trying to impress. Nothing wrong with that. Latin could also come to your aid when things have not gone so well. 'This is where I have my *Zinnia disappointens*,' you say, meaning that the flower did not quite live up to the gorgeous picture on the seed packet. 'And over there you can see my *Delphinium totalis calamitosa*.' We can also admire your *Begonia trampolata feles horribilis Wilkinsonienses* – or, as it is more commonly known, the begonia trampled by the awful cat belonging to the Wilkinsons from next door.

Surplus Veg

These are dangerous times. There you are, sitting and minding your own business in your local, say the Harrow or the Rose and Crown, when somebody you barely know approaches and slips you a cabbage. First thing in the morning you find a bag full of gnarled cooking apples on your doorstep; somebody left it there in the dead of night and then legged it away down the street.

Yes, it is the season when gardeners are offloading their surplus fruit and veg. It is well meaning of them, of course, and it is touching that they are so proud of their produce, but it can leave you with a challenge. (When I hear it has been a bumper year for gooseberries I get a sense of doom, and I have to admit that I'm a reluctant stewer of plums.)

This sudden seasonal munificence is not just a feature of country life. In the towns, at this time, you can spot the allotment holders by the glint in their eye and the bag of lettuces or earthy carrots they are carrying as they walk purposefully towards you.

There are interesting undertones here. I believe a courgette is a useful measure of friendship. If someone gives you small courgettes it's a sign that you are a close and valued friend; if the courgettes are approaching marrow size when you get them, it means the gardener is getting desperate and you are a last resort.

My advice is to be grateful for the runner beans but not too effusive or a tsunami of runner beans will follow, accompanied by desperate cries of 'You can freeze them!' Keep a low profile in the autumn, when vast amounts of green tomatoes are bandied about, with a lot of loose talk of chutney. Above all, be on your guard at all times, or you will find yourself landed with half a hundredweight of quinces.

Talking to Plants

The violas in the tubs on our balcony were extremely put out when I told them what Alan Titchmarsh had said. He had the nerve to tell *Radio Times* that talking to plants has no benefit at all. His mistake, I believe, is to assume that all plants understand English, whereas it is obvious from their names that their preferred language is Latin. Even if you can't actually hold a conversation in Latin you will find most plants benefit if you give them a cheery '*gaudeamus igitur*' in the morning, then perhaps '*o tempora o mores*' round midday and a '*habeas corpus*' last thing at night. Weeds don't understand Latin, so there is no danger of them benefiting from these greetings.

Plants have their own language and you will have more success, for example, if you are fluent in clematis. I'm planning to bring out a book entitled *Learn to Speak Geranium in Seven Days*. (There will be an accompanying CD.) If you are not very good at picking up languages it is still worthwhile to yodel to your alpines. You will notice a marked difference after a week – and an improvement in your yodelling. Don't forget to murmur sweet nothings to

your lilies of the valley, but do not address your compost heap until you have been properly introduced. Remember, when talking to rhododendrons, that they have a very short attention span.

People swear at lawnmowers, chat to their dogs and cats, hamsters and even goldfish. It's also generally considered a good idea to go and tell the bees the latest family news. So why not talk to slugs? This could be the answer to the problem of garden pests. I think you will find, if you address a few well-chosen sarcastic remarks to them, slugs will flee your garden in a matter of hours. Then you can go and jeer at the greenfly.

Dog TV

I have always pictured the owners of Labradors as contented tweedy people living in the nicer country properties – old rectories, perhaps. They put on their Barbours, select a handsome walking stick and go for a leisurely stroll on a Sunday morning, then pop into the pub for a genial drink before lunch. Now I discover that they have a dark secret: their dogs may be couch potatoes, lolling about on the sofa all day with a packet of chews, glued to the box, waiting for the next Andrex commercial to come on.

It is reported that the switch to digital television is making it easier for dogs to follow the images on the screen and their owners have noticed a change in their behaviour. Many dogs, which once ignored the screen, are now watching for fifty minutes a day. A survey suggests that Labradors are the most avid viewers, followed by spaniels and border collies. Soaps are the most popular programmes with dogs, but they are not so keen on noisy game shows. Now when I see a Staffordshire bull terrier panting on its leash, dragging its owner along, I realise it probably just wants to get home to catch up with the latest episode of *Emmerdale*. When I hear barking next door, I imagine the eager Jack Russell, with the TV remote in its mouth, nagging its master for 'watchies'.

This development is going to lead to huge changes in lifestyle. Be prepared for many more programmes with doggie product placement in them; biscuits and beanbags will pop up in every shot. Pet accessory shops will sell dogs' TV dinners and 3D glasses for poodles. It will cause upheavals in the Kennel Club; pointers will be specially bred to identify the killer in *Midsomer Murders* and there will be a Crufts category of working dog which barks to warn you if there is about to be another catastrophe in *EastEnders*.

It will also do wonders for dog-owner snobbery. 'Oh yes,' your upwardly mobile neighbour will say, 'she's a pedigree borzoi and she *insists* on watching *Newsnight* every night.' Meanwhile, some rougher animals will be desperate to appear in downmarket reality shows; just think of the unsavoury things that could happen in the *Big Rover* house.

Eventually all TV programmes will be aimed more at dogs than at humans. Or perhaps that is happening already.

Whisperer

In my youth, living in the country, I used to scratch pigs until they toppled over in bliss – or possibly it was boredom. I've suddenly realised that I could now call myself a pig whisperer and this could be an extremely useful addition to my CV. Come to think of it, I also used to blow into cows' nostrils because it was supposed to tame them. I really ought to be presenting my own top-rating TV show called *The Heifer Soother*.

It's all the rage these days; the country is swarming with horse whisperers and dog whisperers and you can hardly hear yourself think for all the whispering going on. Just the other week we were reading in the papers about the man who claims to be the country's first rabbit whisperer. He treats rabbits with behavioural problems, hypnotising them by massaging their bellies while bowing to them so they don't feel threatened.

I hadn't realised that delinquent bunnies were such a big problem in this country, but it shows that there is still a lot of mileage in whispering. It's a matter of finding the market. Looking for a humane way of getting rid of vermin in your house? Just call in the mouse murmurer who will kneel on the floor and murmur unsettling things down their holes so they have a sudden impulse to pack up and leave.

I'm actually thinking of using my undoubted skills in this area to become a wasp charmer. I could deal with wasps with behavioural problems which lead them to blunder round your living room bumping into things. I'd wear a special sort of antennae headdress to waggle and show empathy with the wasp, then I'd buzz sympathetically to win its trust and persuade it to fly out through the window. As an encore, if you like, I could make your Gloucester Old Spot fall over.

Wasp

Forget about mists and leaves turning to gold; don't talk to me about conkers and bonfires and pumpkins. No, the true essence of autumn is the dozy wasp. This is the season when he crouches on the carpet or clings to the curtain and looks back over his life.

On the whole it has been a good one, he decides. There was the great camaraderie of the nest, of course, and then the joy of getting together with a few mates and performing aerobatics round a picnic. Oh yes, those lovely, lazy summer evenings hanging about dinner parties in gardens, dipping into a glass of wine, then dodging the futile flapping hands of the humans.

Then there was the bliss of the first rotting plum. They say you never forget your first rotting plum, and it's true. In the early days, he could go for hours, banging his head against a window pane, doing a circuit of the room and then banging his head against the window pane again. Those were the days. Now he doesn't get the same buzz from colliding with glass as he used to. There's no thrill in skittering round inside a lampshade, enjoying the warmth of the bulb.

To be honest, he doesn't have the energy for window panes. And he feels the cold. On the whole, he has few regrets. He just wishes, before he goes, he could sting just one more person.

Last week, he got his wish. I felt a tickle on top of my head and I brushed at it. The wasp struck and then lumbered away. On top of the head, where there's hardly any flesh and not much hair, it's specially painful. I sometimes wonder if it has affected my brain. Could it turn me into some kind of monster, half-man, half-wasp? Is this why I have a sudden craving for raspberry jam?

The Good Life

Gordon Ramsay

Admirers of Gordon Ramsay will be interested to learn that I have produced an exciting new recipe book to accompany the television series *Ramsay's Kitchen Nightmares*. The book is a comprehensive guide to the *Sacre Bleu* cookery which he has helped to make so fashionable. Here, taken from the book, is my special recipe for Lamb Cooked with Asterisks:

Break six eggs into a bowl and give them a good bollocking. Set aside. Now lay three lamb epithets on a board and pummel for five minutes. By the end of this process, the lamb should be cowed, but not completely flattened. Take it outside and teach it a good lesson. Bring it back into the kitchen and sprinkle with asterisks, then pointedly ignore.

It is now time to rant the onions and garlic and threaten

the herbs. Place the herbs on another chopping board and bruise them, using your forehead. A little later in the preparation you will know where you can stick them. Grease an oven-proof dish passionately.

Heat some olive oil and a heavy-bottomed effing pan and add the ranted onions. Soften for about fifteen minutes, swearing constantly. At the point where the onions turn a pinkish colour when you yell at them, take the effing pan off the heat and bang it down heavily on a work surface, preferably metal, but marble will do. Allow a few moments for expressions of despair and disbelief. Give a few good shakes of the head and perhaps a shrug or two.

Turn up the heat where the onions were softening and set fire to the corner of the tea towel which should be draped over your left shoulder. Throw the tea towel onto the floor, stamp on it repeatedly until completely incoherent. Check the asterisks and add some more if you think they are needed. Add a good pinch of the charred fragments of tea towel to the onions. Give the mixture a good glare and allow to vituperate.

Take two ripe expletives and, using a blinding knife, slice them thinly, discarding any pieces which are not colourful enough. Place the slices in a food processor and harass. Pour the bollocked egg mixture over the harassed expletive pulp. Whisk violently. Storm out of the kitchen, slamming the door, then return. Eye cleaver dangerously.

Excoriate a leek and denounce a medium-sized bulb of fennel, very roughly chopped, and stir-fry for two minutes. Tell your assistant (if you still have one) where to shove them.

It is now time to embarrass the lamb. Place it in a hot frying pan and sneer at it, about two minutes each side. Get a bloody great saucepan (one that makes a satisfying clang when you hit someone over the head with it) and chuck in the lamb, the onion and tea towel mixture and the leek and fennel.

Take half a Savoy cabbage and give it the four-letter treatment until it starts to wilt, then add it to the pan and place it on the stove. Adjust the asterisks and add freshly ground teeth. Bang a lid on very hard and cook slowly for about forty minutes. After the first twenty minutes, remove the lid and give the mixture a piece of your mind, about the size of your thumb.

You are now going to need a complete roll of kitchen foil. With quick jerking motions, pull the foil off its cardboard holder and, using floured hands, screw it up tightly into sixteen pieces about the size of golf balls. Hurl these at the fridge or at anyone else who may be in the kitchen. Take the cylindrical cardboard part of the roll and use it to belabour a large china mixing bowl for about ten minutes.

By now, the mixture in the pan should have got its act together. Turn up the heat and give it one more harangue. Then transfer everything to a baking dish, add a bouquet garni of blasphemy, profanity and aspersion (and any other herb) and place in the oven at gas mark four. Leave it for twenty minutes, turn the heat up to gas mark seven and cook for a further fifty minutes, lambasting it frequently.

When removing the dish from the oven, some people prefer to use oven gloves, but it is more authentic without. Finish off the dish under the grill, until you are sizzling, and serve with a steaming diatribe or perhaps with a few fresh tirades. After just one mouthful, your guests are bound to declare: 'This is absolute ****.'

Avocado

In a shock move, our local greengrocer has put up a sign in the shop announcing that avocado pears will now be kept behind the till, so, if you want one, a staff member will select a ripe one for you. Clearly, this is a response to a wave of irresponsible avocado-squeezing in the neighbourhood.

It is a sad day for our society when we all have to suffer because of the actions of a few. It is also the thin end of the wedge: the time will surely come when we will no longer be allowed to choose our own kumquats, when the freshly cooked beetroot are kept in a locked cabinet and leek police patrol the shop.

I have a pretty good idea about who these avocado-abusers are. They are the same people who spill a Maris Piper and would rather kick it along the aisle than pick it up; they are the ones who furtively redistribute the strawberries between punnets and pull two bananas off a bunch. They probably also tear too many brown paper bags from the string and then leave the surplus ones scattered over the display of tomatoes.

It would not surprise me to learn that these perpetrators of fruit and veg crime also sneak round the shop slyly inserting apostrophes in the wrong place on the price labels, just so they can sneer at the innocent greengrocer. Where did these people go wrong? It probably started with grapefruit-sniffing and then it was downhill from there.

The staff at our local greengrocer's must be expert at avocado-squeezing; they probably went on a course; there is probably a diploma in avocado-squeezing. If there is, these people have got it made and the world is their Galia melon. They are urgently needed in supermarkets where, at present, avocados (and peaches and pears) are marked 'Perfectly Ripe' and remain rock hard for the next ten days.

Barbecue

Do you speak barbecue? As we are about to enter the season of outdoor meals it's important to be sure you have mastered the language. Here's an example of a useful phrase: 'Hisso hovey to ee ow.' Obviously, this means 'It's so lovely to eat out.' The basic principle of the barbecue language is that, when you have a mouth full of burning hot sausage, you must avoid using hard consonants and make maximum use of the letter 'h'. The great thing about the letter 'h' is that it enables you to blow on the sausage while retaining it in your mouth.

The letter 'w' is also useful – as in an urgent request for a cold drink: 'Hould I wossibly have a wass of waher?'

See if you can translate the following exchange:

> *'Why are woo weebing? Are woo unhawwwy abou*
> *   somewing?'*
> *'No, I jus have warbecue moke in my weyes.'*
> *'Oh, would woo ike anower hossage? Or a wurger?'*
> *'No, jussa anower wass of waher.'*
> *'Did woo know woo have mato hetchup all dow*
> *   your shir?'*

Mime also plays a vital part in the barbecue language, as it removes the risk that you may spit out a mouthful of coleslaw or a chunk of marinated chicken drumstick. Cardboard plates are not much good for holding food but useful for signalling. Waving a plate at arm's length in an anti-clockwise direction means: 'Look out, you are about to kick over my glass of wine which is on the ground next to me.' Throwing three plates in the air sends the message: 'Help! I can't get out of this deckchair.'

Here's another mime to look out for: if someone cups their right hand just beneath their chin and waves their left hand, as if flapping at an imaginary wasp, it means: 'I can't stop now. I have to go and spit this piece of steak gristle into that flower bed over there.'

Cookery Lessons

School reports could become more interesting now that the Education Secretary has decided to make cookery classes compulsory:

'Mmmm ... wow ... that is just incredible ... the texture is amazing and the apple in the *tarte tatin* really comes through. Jennifer's work this term has been yummy.'

'It is a measure of Trevor's difficulties with cookery that, on three or four occasions this term, the dog has refused to eat his homework. Trevor must learn that there is more involved in preparing a nutritious meal than swearing, even though, in this particular area, he has proved to be remarkably inventive.'

'Fiona continues to struggle with the slotted spoon and has still not mastered the garlic press, but she is making great strides with her scrambled egg. Well done, Fiona, for winning the Delia Smith Prize for Effort.'

'Notice to parents: the Home Economics Department has been closed since the fire of last March. Miss Wilberforce hopes to be able to resume cookery classes in the summer term in 2014 when she will be getting pupils to have another go at *crêpes suzette.*'

'Darren has been rather out of his depth in cookery. I think the main reason is that he was under the mistaken impression that he was attending metalwork lessons. On a brighter note, Mr Mortimer, the head of metalwork, says the welding in Darren's Victoria sponge was first class.'

'I'd like to take this opportunity to remind Tania that frozen ready meals and microwaves are not permitted in GCSE exams. In her course work Tania was let down by her pot noodle module.'

'Another outstanding term's work by Luke. I gave him a straight A for his boar's head brawn and his lobster thermidor went down very well at the parents' evening. Perhaps it is now time to tackle some more basic dishes, as we have had to sell the playing fields to a property developer to cover the cost of Luke's ingredients.'

Dipping

I am actually rather sorry that the EU, faced with general ridicule, changed its mind about banning restaurants from serving olive oil in dipping bowls. The eurocrats should have stuck to their directives and even reinforced the ban with swingeing sanctions.

Don't you think that a dipping bowl is really an unnecessary bit of spraunce? When the waiter puts it on the table, I get the message: 'As you are going to have to wait a considerable time for your food, here's something for you to play with in the meantime. And to make you feel a bit posher, we've put a little puddle of balsamic vinegar in the middle of the pool of olive oil. You will notice also that we have swirled the balsamic vinegar to make a rather pretty pattern.'

Somehow you feel you're expected to dip into the dipping bowl, just to prove you are unfazed and you know the ropes. In other restaurants it's perfectly OK to leave the butter dish untouched, but the dipping bowl is part of the ritual. Only a recklessly brave person would say: 'Could you take this oily pool away and bring me a slab of Kerrygold?'

Anyway, dipping, in general, is an inelegant business. Somebody at a party twisting a Pringle round a bowl to collect the maximum load of guacamole is not a pretty sight. Watching that load making its perilous journey to the mouth is equally unsettling. And what are you supposed to do with the rest of your naked stick of celery after you have eaten the blob of hummus on the end of it? Wave it around as a sort of conversational aid? What is the rule about dipping it into the hummus again? These are troubling questions.

On the subject of tiresome accessories on restaurant tables, I've never been entirely happy with finger bowls. The trouble is, I usually forget to use this receptacle of tepid water which has been placed in front of me, along with the mussels or the artichoke. When the waiter returns to collect the debris, the water in the bowl is still perfectly clear. He must suspect I've been wiping my sticky fingers on the tablecloth. Sometimes I just manage a quick dabble, as an afterthought, just to make the water cloudy.

Here's an idea: I propose that the EU should ban restaurant finger bowls. On health and safety grounds, of course.

Food Talk

Programmes about competitive cooking, like *Masterchef* and *The Great British Bake Off*, may not affect our own performance in the kitchen, but they have certainly transformed the way we talk about food. Once upon a time, after the first mouthful, we would say 'mmmmm' or even 'yummy' (or sometimes 'bleah'), but now we gaze into the middle distance, ponder for eleven seconds and then say: 'That Bisto comes through very nicely,' or 'The sausage works really well.' We may also observe that a small pool of HP sauce on the edge of the plate would 'lift' the presentation. At breakfast, we remark on the nice contrast in textures between the charred and the pale areas of the slice of toast.

Meanwhile, in the kitchen, it is an emotional roller coaster. 'Grilled lamb chops,' we say, 'it doesn't get any tougher than this.' We almost swoon with relief and say, 'I can't believe they said they really liked my frozen peas.' And, yes, there are tears when the oven glove catches fire. When we fall down on our cottage pie we vow: 'I'm going to give my apple crumble my everything.' We are passionate about fish fingers and we know we are going to have to raise our game with our mashed potato. It has become a mountain to climb.

The family, seated round the dining table, are impatient for their meal. 'You've got just ten more minutes,' they call out, and then, far too soon, they yell: 'Time's up! Step away from your toad in the hole.'

At the end of the meal we stand nervously by the stove, holding the still-smouldering oven glove, while the rest of the family go into a huddle. 'As you know,' their spokeswoman says, 'we're going to have to say goodbye to one person this week, and that person is . . . you.' Then we all hug like anything and the washing-up gets forgotten.

Hotel Breakfast

We have just got back from a couple of days away so I have several pages of notes for my treatise on *The True Meaning of the Hotel Breakfast*. This is a guide to the secret rituals and the subtle hypocrisies of that whispering world, tackling such dilemmas as 'the buffet table – clockwise or anti-clockwise?' and 'toast – brown or white?'

Of course, when the waitress asks you the toast question the correct answer is 'mixed'. Why on earth do we say this? We don't have mixed toast at home. Are we

nervous of appearing too dogmatic on the toast-hue issue in public?

Some hotel breakfasts now feature a toast-making machine. This is usually commandeered by one male guest who stands over it while its hot little conveyor belt delivers the end product painfully slowly. This man is determined to have fourteen slices of toast (mixed, of course) before he lets you near the machine.

Meanwhile the Full English Breakfast is far too genteel to call itself the Fry-Up. To make guests feel it's the healthy choice the menu tells us that the eggs were laid less than a hundred yards down the road and it gives you the name of the farmer who produced the bacon and the (always award-winning) sausages.

My experience is that very few people have the *full* Full English Breakfast. That would be greedy, so there's always a respectable opt-out. We ask for the 'cooked' breakfast then add primly 'but without the black pudding and the tomato'. This makes it all right.

Now for the buffet table. The golden rule is: 'Don't Trust the Clockwise Woman'. She is the one who has picked all the strawberries out of the fruit salad, finished the orange juice and is about to nick a banana for later. She will pop it into her handbag, along with the shower gel and the sewing kit.

Photos of Food

We used to have to go to great lengths to avoid the holiday photographs of friends, but nowadays these same friends want to show us pictures of a delicious *spaghetti puttanesca* they ate recently or a magnificent sea bream they ordered in a restaurant. Everybody is at it, photographing their food, posting the pictures on Facebook or emailing them to friends. Even my wife does it, but she is merely taking photographs of the puddings I order so she can use them as Exhibits, A, B and C when I am prosecuted for offences under the Abuse of Waistline Act.

My daughter was in a smart restaurant recently where the people at every single table were taking pictures of their food. She told me this while showing me images on her iPad of all the dishes in the tasting menu she had ordered.

Actually, not every single dish, because one or two were so delicious she wolfed them down before she had a chance to point her camera at them. She could have filled in those gaps by photographing those at other tables, but she has been too well brought up.

I've heard of one case where someone in a restaurant was asked by perfect strangers if they could take a picture of her pudding. (Apparently dry ice was involved.) Important etiquette questions arise, now that so much attention is paid to the appearance of food. Is it acceptable to rearrange the items on the plate to make a better picture? Maybe to move the thin slices of radish closer to the pea shoots and redistribute the sweetbreads? Could you order an extra anchovy to improve the composition? Should restaurants start offering a special photogenic menu?

Soon I expect to see someone leaning back after the main course, giving a contented sigh and saying: 'Nothing more for me, thanks. My camera's memory card is completely full up.'

Roast Potato Wars

A certain queasiness has set in, as we are already faced with countless colour photographs of implausibly gleaming roast turkeys and geese, and self-assured famous chefs pontificating on how to prepare the 'perfect' Christmas dinner.

So it was a relief to see there has been an attempt to stir up some controversy over the all-important question of roast potatoes. Nigella Lawson is a champion of goose fat for crispiness, while Heston Blumenthal favours beef dripping as 'the vital ingredient in creating something extraordinary'. The only way to resolve this crucial issue is, as Harry Hill would say, 'Fight!' There must be scuffles in the street as Nigella supporters, with banners, clash with grim-faced Blumenthal disciples. Militant pro-parboilers must go on the march, chanting their slogans.

Passions could also be aroused over the matter of whether to cut a little X at the base of every single Brussels sprout. I see Rick Stein and Delia Smith in a tense stand-off over this one, with Delia uttering words she may later regret. I see Gordon Ramsay stopping strangers in the street, jabbing them in the chest and saying: 'Stuffing. Cavity or neck? Where do you stand?' I predict riots in the gourmet district of Chichester, stirred up by Mary Berry's pronouncements on giblet gravy. I fear innocent vegetarians in Harrogate may be caught up in unrest over something Nigel Slater said about bacon rolls. Celebrity chefs are always talking about 'passion', so it's time to be passionate about bread sauce. Nutmeg or no nutmeg? I call upon the Hairy Bikers to stand up and be counted on this one.

Meanwhile, I am gathering a small group of zealots and desperadoes round me, to support me in my own passionate campaign. We march under a banner which says: 'Death to the Honey-Glazed Parsnip!' We are currently debating about whether to hold James Martin hostage, to draw attention to our cause.

Breakfast

There is a mystique about breakfast and I think this is why there has been such grief at the news that marmalade is losing out in popularity to peanut butter and chocolate spread. Alas, the ideal breakfast exists only in our imagination. Hotels are perpetuating the myth with their Full English Breakfast.

This is nothing like the *real* English breakfast, which is taken on the run – a yoghurt in the bathroom, a takeaway coffee for the sprint down the street and an apple on the bus. While we dream of chunky marmalade and lightly boiled eggs, the real English breakfast is a matter of high-speed improvisation.

I'm thinking of opening an hotel, so I can offer the Authentic Breakfast Experience. Here's the menu:

'May we suggest you begin your meal with a quick swig of flat ginger ale and one of our special past-their-best bananas or a home-bruised peach? After that you can choose a chunk of cold blackberry and apple pie from last night's dinner, accompanied by one of our selection of gourmet cold custards. All this comes with toast, scraped to your liking.

'Alternatively, you may wish to visit our de luxe buffet and avail yourself of the dregs of a beetroot smoothie, a hot cross bun spread with Marmite or some salt and vinegar crisps which have been matured on the plate so that they no longer have that tiresome and noisy crispness. Coffee in cardboard beakers will be served as you leave.'

Those of us who bewail marmalade's decline can comfort ourselves that, in twenty years, tetchy old chaps will be writing to the newspapers complaining: 'What has happened to good old peanut butter? In my day you could get lovely crunchy stuff in proper screw-top jars, but now it's all smooth and bland. I search in vain for traditional chocolate spread, but I find it has given way to tomato ketchup.'

Clearing the Table

One of the bonus pleasures of eating out in a restaurant is the spectacle of the waitress (or waiter) clearing the table after the main course. They pile up all your dirty plates, used and unused cutlery, side dishes, empty bottles and half-eaten rolls into a thrillingly precarious mountain and, just as you think it must all noisily collapse, they add the salt and pepper and the butter dish to the summit. And most of them are smiling while they perform this feat, and asking if you enjoyed your meal.

You'd think it would be simpler to make two or three trips to do this, but it is obviously some part of the waiters' code of honour that the table must be cleared in one go. The process requires such specialised skill and creates such a level of suspense that it really ought to be an Olympic event. The Chinese would walk away with the gold medal, of course. A Chinese waiter is always able to clear away a phenomenal number of multi-shaped dishes and a dangerous amount of awkward leftovers – but you don't always get the smile.

Clearing the table could be an event in a revised version of the modern pentathlon. The existing modern pentathlon consists of fencing, a 200m freestyle swim,

show jumping, a three-kilometre run and pistol shooting. It was introduced at the 1912 Olympics, so it's not all that modern now.

What other four sports could we combine with table clearing? Just off the top of my head, I can think of freestyle stuffing a duvet into its cover, opening the packaging of a Marks and Spencer sandwich against the clock, picking up 3,500 polystyrene worms from the floor and putting them back in a box, and an artistic routine demonstrating Sellotape skills.

I must run the idea past the International Olympic Committee; I'll invite them out to lunch.

Spa

We have just spent a night at a spa hotel in West Sussex. Great comfort and lovely gardens. The only trouble was, every time I met a member of the staff in the corridor they would solicitously ask, 'How are you?' I was soon struggling to come up with a suitably spa-ish reply. Rejuvenated? Tingling? Exfoliated? Glowing? And there was running water about the place, designed to soothe but, in my case, just reminding me of the gutters back home. I couldn't believe that drifting about in a hotel in a white bathrobe, with flip-flops and a look of dreamy serenity, was really *me*.

The pampering we chose to experience was in the restaurant, so we resisted the infusions, floats, marinades, thermal stone massage and mud detox. I was briefly tempted by the idea of the Go Guy Male Executive Facial, at £75 for fifty-five minutes. This was mainly because I was curious to find out about the so-called Power Breakfast Mask. Could this be one where the cucumber slices were replaced by slices of bacon or croissant crumbs? Would it all fall off when I tried to drink from my power cup of coffee?

I always enjoy inspecting the paraphernalia on offer in hotel bathrooms. This one had a tube of face and body balm called 'Peace Be Still' and there was also a white square object, whose label announced that it was an Aromatic Cleansing Bar. (What was once called washing is now cleansing; it makes the process sound so Biblical.)

After we got back home, rested and a pound or two heavier, I checked in our local shops for the thing that is used for cleansing. I found a Beauty Cream Bar, an Ivory Bar, something called Gentle Care and countless liquid face, hand and body washes. So it's clear: in many quarters these days 'soap' is now considered a dirty word.

Family Life

Buggies

Am I in danger of turning into a young mother? Lately, as I have been taking my middle grandson (two and three-quarters) for walks, I notice that I have started exchanging little private smiles with the other mothers pushing their prams. I assumed this was just shared maternal pride, but it could be mutual admiration of the brilliant range of pushchairs, buggies and strollers out on the pavements these days. We send silent messages: 'I see you have the nippy Bugaboo with the denim upholstery. They're ideal for town. As you observe, I am pushing the latest little number from Mamas & Papas. She goes like a bomb and folds like a dream, but I'm thinking I might invest in an Urban Single Three-Wheeler, or possibly the Pliko Pramette, which has bags of torque.'

There are so many to marvel at. A particular favourite of mine is the pram in which the child is very high off the ground and facing the pusher; this is the toddler equivalent of the eye-level grill.

The other day, I took this grandson to the playground and, while we pushed the swings, another mother and I exchanged thoughts on various issues like the good local nursery schools and how many mornings a week a child should go. I was doing awfully well and if I had lingered by the climbing frame a little longer I think she would have invited me to join her group of mothers and toddlers who gather in Starbucks most mornings.

It was not to be. I was called away to feed the ducks on the lake. This involves hurling chunks of bread in a desperate effort to fend off the pushy North London geese and then making a run for it. After that, the grandson and I took a nonchalant stroll and ended up spending twenty very happy minutes dropping small bits of gravel, one by one, through a grating. It's a chap thing.

Children in Pubs

Children are quite at home in pubs these days. When I was young we had to hang about outside with a bottle of lemonade, a soggy straw and a packet of Quavers, sometimes daring to peep through a crack in the door at the mysterious adult world of the saloon bar.

The other day I went into a local pub for a quick lunchtime beer and had to wait because the barman was busy fetching an ice bucket then filling it with hot water so that a baby's bottle could be served at just the right temperature.

Sunday lunchtime in the pub is now a family affair – as the Camerons have shown us. The children sit with all their relations tucking into the asparagus quiche, while mothers call for more high chairs to be brought and the younger siblings give an occasional shriek from the ranks of prams blocking the route to the Gents. We unaccompanied adults sit uneasily in the darker corners.

I have a theory that children are gradually turning into the pub bores of our age. We will soon see them leaning against the bar, rocking on their heels and telling knock-knock jokes. That yell from the pram over there is just little Theo saying, 'It's my shout.'

'So, Molly, what buggy are you riding at the moment? Do you still have that old Maclaren Stroller?'

'No, traded it in for a micro-scooter. Lovely silver finish. Goes like a dream. It now takes me seven and three-quarter minutes door-to-door to get to playgroup.'

'Two more cranberry juices and a packet of Skittles, please, barman. And have one yourself.'

'Anyone fancy a game of paper, stone and scissors?'

I see the day coming when the few remaining adults will take up smoking again and huddle on the pavement, occasionally peeping through the crack in the door at the mysterious world of the carousing tots inside.

Family Tree

The way things are going, pretty soon every adult in this country will have done extensive research into his or her family tree. What will we all talk about then? We'll be handing round blurred photocopies of parish records in copperplate handwriting, showing off ancient censuses and bandying the great-great-great-greats. We'll all have a photograph of our bearded Victorian ancestor,

posing stiff-backed with his dutiful wife and thirteen sad-eyed children. (Have you noticed how all bearded Victorian ancestors look the same?)

Family trees provide ideal material for one-upmanship, and the smart thing – as may be seen in all those TV programmes where celebrities explore their past – is to have forebears who have suffered. You need to be descended from a seamstress who died of consumption or a washerwoman who was struck down in the scarlet fever epidemic of 1804. Every family tree must contain a man called Jack who was transported to Australia.

From now on, the chap who used to brag about his new car will announce to his friends: 'My great-great-great-great-uncle on my mother's side was a journeyman goose-strangler. That probably explains why I've always had an ambivalent attitude towards geese.'

A useful tip, when looking into your family's past, is to seek out a young Italian (or possibly French) woman who came to Britain as a singer a couple of centuries ago. This will enable you to claim that you have a fiery and passionate nature. Also, it's always useful if you can dredge up a bigamist.

Now, of course, we have the DNA craze. This is going to be really big. Next time someone boasts to me that they are distantly related to a midshipman who was lost overboard off the coast of Gibraltar in 1719, I'll tell them that the nearest matches for my DNA are a tribe in the Amazon rainforest and a breed of vole found only in small area in Norway.

Gramping

This year three-quarters of British families with young children intend to go gramping – that is, going on holiday with the grandparents. This is supposed to save on childcare costs and keep family members in touch.

As a grandparent, I would strongly advise against this; it just adds to the anxieties and responsibilities of the grandchildren, who have to be on high alert all the time. Every minute it's 'Don't go too close to the edge of the pool, Granny', and 'Grandpa, we're not stopping now. Remember, I *asked* you before we set out in the car if you wanted to go.'

Here are some of the other annoying things grandparents do on holiday: they get up too early in the morning and fidget; they set out all their pills in a line on the breakfast table; they talk to strangers in hotel lifts, or they befriend the people in the holiday cottage next door so that you have to spend more time with them than you would wish. They get lost and are finally found in a church or a churchyard, reading gravestones. They can devote forty minutes to choosing a suitable postcard to send to some person they hardly know.

In the car, they can never manage the seat-belts and have to get a child to help; then for the whole journey they make the windows go up and down and ask 150 times, 'Is that all right for you in the back?'

Grandparents are deeply shocked by the price of ice creams, then buy a cornet with three scoops in the most exotic flavours and immediately spill them down their front. They specialise in embarrassing sun hats.

In the evening, while the parents go out to dinner in some exciting restaurant the children have to stay behind and babysit the grandparents. If I were going on holiday I certainly wouldn't take *me*.

Granny Tax

There has been a great deal written about the so-called Granny Tax. This is George Osborne's Budget announcement that he is freezing the age-related allowance for pensioners. It has been fiercely attacked, but it has given me a brilliant idea: why doesn't he impose a *proper* granny tax? That is, a levy on every family which has a granny.

Grandma represents a benefit in kind. She provides free child-minding and babysitting services, dispenses traditional medical advice and wise sayings and is often the supplier of knitted garments and peppermints. I propose a tax of £50 per gran. Two-granny families pay double, of course, and in families where remarriages occur there may be even three or four grandmotherly sources of revenue. The beauty of the idea is that as our population ages the supply of grannies increases, generating even more money for the Exchequer.

Of course, there will always be people who try to avoid this levy. Let us hope they won't follow the example of our ancestors with the window tax and brick granny up. Mr Osborne may have to take action to close the loophole of offshore grannies who are registered in the Bahamas or hidden in the vaults of Swiss banks. There is also a danger that grandma could be turned into a limited company or floated on the Stock Exchange.

HMRC will also have to set up an investigations branch to track down undeclared grannies. Detector vans will tour the streets with sophisticated electronic devices that can pick up sounds of cooing. Shopkeepers will be obliged to report any ladies buying photograph albums, and police will monitor unusual migrations of elderly female persons at Christmas.

This granny levy will prove such a goldmine that the Chancellor will be able to reduce the rate of income tax for top earners even further, to 25 per cent.

I commend this measure to the House.

Micro-scooters

After studying the subject for a long time, I have come to the conclusion that young children are desperate to own a micro-scooter, but they don't want to ride it. A child regards the scooter as an essential accessory for his or her parents to carry; it is a symbol of the child's authority.

I see them every morning as they troop past our flat on the way to the local (most desirable) primary school. The child meanders along behind as the mother marches ahead, pushing the buggy and carrying the scooter. She is also carrying a rucksack containing various emergency snacks the child may require at any moment and the child's homework, a fragile and unwieldy model of a farmyard.

The mother is also talking on her mobile phone to another mother, making arrangements to pick up the other mother's child after school – plus micro-scooter and splodgy painting of something or other and violin – and take him or her home for more emergency snacks.

At weekends the child will reluctantly mount the micro-scooter – but not to scoot. The child stands on the scooter so that the father has to bend over, hold the handlebars and push and steer. That is why scooters are micro: to make fathers bend. A child instinctively knows that a man without a stoop is not a proper father. Finally the child agrees to scoot the scooter himself. This is to embarrass the father. At weekends I see men sprinting down the pavement in pursuit of a dot on the horizon, yelling: 'Stop when you get to the road, Alfie!'

I am going to suggest to the local desirable primary school that at their next sports day they have a Mothers and Scooters race – with the mothers carrying the scooters, of course, plus rucksacks of emergency snacks and a splodgy painting. While talking on a mobile phone, needless to say.

Mothers' Questions

We are told that, on average, mothers have to answer twenty-three questions an hour.

They have to deal with all their children's queries, such as 'Why is water wet?' and 'What are shadows made of?' and 'Is God married?' I can quite believe this statistic is accurate, but I think we ought to spare a thought for poor children, whose days are spent under a hail of questions from their mothers. Your average small child hardly has any time to find an original place to hide his shoe, as he (or she) copes with a constant flow of interrogation.

What have you got stuck up your nose? Do you need the loo? Have you been good? Well, where were you when you last had Mr Hippo? Did you make your sister cry? Where did you learn that word? Do you think Daddy really likes Brygida?

You are having a thoughtful sit on the loo and every twenty seconds she is hovering over you with more questions. Have you done anything? Shall I have a look? Do you want to try again later?

It seems that mothers are in constant need of reassurance. Why did you draw me with three noses and fangs? Why is T Rex in the butter? What did you bury in that hole in the garden? Is Brygida nice to Daddy? What is that smell?

Then there are those impossible hypothetical or philo-sophical questions. How could Mr Hippo have drawn on the wall with his felt tip pen when we don't even know where Mr Hippo is? If I let you watch the *Wallace and Gromit* DVD one more time, make you finish only half your peas, promise that we will make more chocolate crunchies tomorrow, think seriously about getting a guinea pig and let you keep your wellies on, will you go to bed? What makes you think your socks are sad? If Mr Tumble, Stegosaurus, the Queen, next door's dog and a worm can't come to your birthday party, who would you like to invite instead? Why won't you ever go to sleep?

Your average small boy may consider himself pretty well informed about dinosaurs and the names of the rolling stock associated with *Thomas the Tank Engine*, but sometimes his mother seems to think he is omniscient. Where are my house keys? Why is my mobile in the fridge? Why isn't the goldfish in his bowl? What have I done to deserve this?

Packing the Boot

I so enjoy the August street theatre of people loading their car boots for the summer holiday. Sometimes the whole family is involved; each member, in turn, brings his or her contribution to the rear of the car, puts it inside, then, in a spirit of constructive criticism, takes out the bags other people have placed there and rearranges them. The next person arrives and repeats the process. One case is deemed unworthy of a place in the boot and is dumped on the back seat. Then it's back in the boot. Eventually, a consensus is achieved; they give the luggage a final pat, the boot is ceremoniously closed, they get in the car and they drive off.

Other families simply hurl armfuls of clothes, blankets, wellington boots and overflowing rucksacks onto the back seat and then chuck the children (still in pyjamas) into any space that is left.

Often one parent (usually the father, I'm afraid) takes command. The wife and children are pale faces at the window of the house as he attaches that bossy pod to the roof of the car. Then perhaps they gather round as he loads the boot. Like a surgeon calling for his scalpels, he names the cases that must be passed to him: 'Black suitcase with strap . . . red zip bag . . . cardboard box . . . brown suitcase . . . bike . . . straw hat . . . Sainsbury's bag . . .'

If it's a minicab taking them to the airport, the driver becomes a spectator as they arrange their various pieces of baggage. It's clear that there is a special kind of car boot feng shui and if the holdall is placed in the wrong spot in relation to the Antler suitcase, disaster will strike the holiday. Finally, everything is in place, they get in the cab and drive off, leaving one lightweight fold-up luggage trolley behind on the pavement. If you look very closely you could actually imagine that it is waving goodbye to them.

Wedding Photos

We went to a lovely wedding last weekend and I played my usual part as 'you on the end'. At some point, the official photographer, taking the group picture, will shout: 'You on the end, sir, can you move in a bit?' That's me. On the end, wishing I'd put my glass down before I'd joined the line-up. In wedding albums all over the country, the man on the end with a vague look and the empty glass is probably me.

It's such a performance. The photographer has to think up groups of more and more ingenious combinations of guests. 'Right, now we'll have bridesmaids' mothers, with groom's nephews and best man's cousins,' he announces. 'OK, all stepfathers line up now, with groom's former girlfriends and all grannies who have not yet been photographed,' he commands. 'Now I just need the caterers, the vicar's dog and those people who just happened to be passing by.'

You have to sympathise with the official photographers because they are now competing with all the guests and their digital cameras. These people have the single-minded ruthless approach of cameramen waiting outside nightclubs for semi-celebrities. The swarm of aunts and cousins with little cameras can be relentless in the pursuit of a wedding picture. I call them the digirazzi. They prowl at family occasions, hunting in packs. Suddenly there is a forest of arms in the air as Canons and Panasonics are held aloft to capture the moment.

All this might even inspire the official photographer to think up an entirely new group. 'Let's have one last picture of groom's ushers with Olympus camcorders and members of the bride's family who have Nikons.' There's also that popular shot when the men attempt to throw their top hats up into the sky in unison. Someone ought to try that with everyone chucking their digital cameras high in the air.

That's Life

Air Travel

Ladies and gentlemen, my name is Sandra and I will be your senior in-cabin amenities co-ordinator on this flight to Malaga, or wherever. My team and I would like to welcome you on board and thank you for choosing to fly with Supersoar Airlines – even if you didn't really have a choice. Still, my team and I have to put on a brave face about wearing this apricot-coloured uniform, so the least you can do is accept the inevitable with some grace.

While we are still boarding this plane, can I, at this point, ask a passenger in Row 12 to stand up and rearrange all his personal items in his overhead locker for a long time, while sticking his backside out into the aisle and stopping other people squeezing past and reaching their seats? If everybody is seated too early people will start expecting this plane to take off.

Our estimated hanging-about-on-the-tarmac time today is approximately 105 minutes. You may wish to put your watches back one hour now so that our take-off time will not seem quite so badly behind schedule.

In a few minutes the tinkly piped music in the background will be drowned by the roar and hiss of the ventilation system. This is quite normal and there is no cause for optimism that something is actually about to happen.

Cabin staff are now about to move down the aircraft making all the people who have hand luggage under their seats put it in the overhead lockers provided, and all passengers who have bags in the lockers will be ordered to put them under the seat.

My colleague Patsy is about to come round offering copies of last Thursday's *Frankfurter Allgemeine Zeitung,* which is the only newspaper we could get hold of because of some mix-up with our suppliers. If there is anybody on board who reads German, I would ask them at this time to identify themselves and look a bit pleased.

It may be of interest to you to know that our late-arriving passenger should be coming on board in about two minutes. He will be wearing a Panama hat, a pale linen suit and a smug expression. He will be carrying two gigantic suitcases which he will bump against the shoulders of those of you in aisle seats until he reaches his own place which is at the rear of the aircraft.

Your pilot today is Captain Roderick Wildblood. In half an hour he will address you in his rich, soothing voice to apologise for the delayed departure. In the meantime we are taxi-ing to a different area of the tarmac so that we can get a better view of those planes which have been lucky enough to be cleared for take-off. Captain Wildblood has also just changed the note of the engines to raise your expectations.

If passengers on the left side of the aircraft look out of the windows they can see the brown suitcase which fell off the baggage handlers' trolley and is now being ignored as it lies on the ground. Passengers on the right side can see a mechanic staring at the wing and shaking his head.

My colleague Trish will now move down the cabin taking coats and belongings at random from the overhead lockers and placing them in other overhead lockers as far away from their owners as possible. At the same time Patsy will, for the 38th time, twitch the curtain which separates the First Class cabin to make sure that nobody in the tourist section gets an unauthorised glimpse of it.

You may like to know that there are now two mechanics staring at our starboard wing and gesticulating.

Ladies and gentleman, as it is nearly time for Captain Wildblood to deliver his apology for the delay, I would ask you now to fold away your trays, put your seats in an upright position and see that your seatbelt is securely fastened so that Patsy can come down the aircraft and glare severely at your groin area. At the same time Trish will open all the overhead lockers and slam them shut very violently.

In a minute I will be demonstrating the Safety Procedure, which I find extremely embarrassing – especially the bit where I have to pretend to blow into the tube to inflate the lifejacket should it fail to inflate automatically. You will find a safety leaflet in the back of the seat. Please study it closely while I am doing the demonstration, so that I don't catch your eye.

As soon as we have taken off, the cabin crew will be wheeling trolleys into the aisle to block your way to the toilets.

Bespoke

The word 'bespoke' has a charming old-fashioned ring to it, suggesting courtly gentlemen's tailors with tape measures round their necks. Suddenly the word is everywhere. You can have bespoke kitchens (they mean fitted) or even bespoke hotels (where the beds are made to measure, I suppose) plus bespoke jewellery and bespoke bicycles.

The other great buzz-word is 'artisan'. To me, it suggests a gnarled old craftsman bent over a workbench fashioning something out of wood. Hang on a minute, here's someone advertising artisan luxury chocolates; surely they haven't been carved with a mallet and chisel? I've come across artisan jewellery (as worn by gnarled old craftsmen?), artisan fireplaces and showers and artisan hairdressers (staffed by wizened old sheep shearers, I expect) plus artisan biscuits, which, to me, summon up a picture of women in shawls spinning custard creams in their cottages.

Then there's artisan bread, of course. This means it's expensive and no artisan could afford it. I wonder if they have loaves pre-sliced by craftsmen.

As selling points, these words seem to have overtaken 'organic', because everything is now supposedly organic, and you don't see 'ethical' about quite so often these days. And 'cheap' doesn't seem to do it any more.

'Locally sourced' is still very popular. Next time you get on your bespoke bicycle to go to the shop to buy your artisan luxury chocolates, make sure you ask if they are locally sourced. A few years ago 'Mrs' and 'Aunt' were all the rage. If you bought chutney it had to be Mrs So-and-So's traditional country chutney and after that you could always pick up a jar of Aunt Matilda's butterscotch. I suppose poor Mrs So-and-So and Aunt Matilda have now lost their jobs and been replaced by artisans. You have to move with the times.

At my age, I still remember when everything was 'morning gathered'. I'd like a morning gathered bespoke kitchen, please.

Country Lore

There is a quaint old country saying which goes, 'You're never more than 150 yards from a hog roast.' It expresses a profound truth, as the number of roadside signs advertising hog roasts is nearly as great as the number of signs announcing boot fairs.

The origins of the summer hog roast are now lost in the mists of the 1990s, though some folklore experts claim they derive from 'hag roasts' when local witches would entice their victims away from church on a Sunday by promising huge lunches of roast meat with giant Yorkshire puddings.

Boot fairs were originally kicking contests. The young men of the village would put on their special hob-nailed boots and gather in a nearby field and kick each other on the shins. The village maidens would gather to watch the sport. At the end of three hours' strenuous kicking, the winner, or 'King Toe-cap', would be proclaimed and he would earn the right to the best parking space in the village. Nowadays, the event has been watered down, and kicking has been replaced by haggling.

In ancient times the most respected figure in the rural community was the man who owned the shop selling TV sets and computers. Once a year the village people would gather so he could test his sound equipment. He would repeat: 'Testing, testing, testing, one, two, three', a few times, then everyone would wander off again. The custom is still kept alive and is known as a fête.

There are still many strange superstitions in the countryside, and there are secret societies that an outsider will never comprehend. If you venture down a country lane you will see signs saying 'BBQ' or 'PYO'. Their meaning is not known, but they are believed to refer to rival 'computer whisperers' who claim to have the power to give faster broadband. A stranger would be well advised not to meddle in such matters.

Fayre

Why the Y? We are now well into the season of acute irritation for pedants like me. It's almost as bad as hay fever. I'm talking about the so-called Summer Fayre, which you see advertised on gate-posts, parish notice boards, on roundabouts and at road junctions and everywhere you turn.

If you look the word up in the dictionary, you will find it is a 'pseudo-archaic spelling of fair'. So the fayre is a pseudo event. The suggestion is that it will be a traditional medieval romp, with roisterous fun, pitchforking bumpkins over hay-carts, chasing wenches round the maypole and guessing how many gallons of mead the squire can drink. In reality, it is stalls of dreaded bric-a-brac, over-iced cupcakes, crockery smashing, a dodgy sound system, a raffle, clouds of smoke from barbecuing sausages, a game of bowls and, if you're lucky, a chaotic dog show.

(Even worse for us pedants are those dire three words 'traditional pub fayre'. It's another way of saying micro-waved chilli con carne and mass-produced meat pies.)

Actually, we went to a Summer Fayre in Norfolk the other weekend and it was fun. There were vintage cars (not medieval ones) on show and we ate soft ice cream out of a tap in the rain, inhaled the barbecue smoke, failed to smash crockery, watched a display of tiny children performing martial arts and resisted the bric-a-brac. There was also an excellent dog show. In the obedience trials all the dogs sat before their owners had a chance to say 'sit' and if there had been a Most Bored in Show category there would have been stiff competition for that rosette. In fact, it was just what a good dog show should be. A perfect day out – apart from the spelling. For next year's Summer Fayre, I a suggest a new game: Throwing the Dictionary at the Organisers.

Hugs

As it's Valentine's Day tomorrow, this would be a good time to mention that the average hug lasts three seconds. Researchers at Dundee University's School of Psychology have established this after analysing the post-competition embraces of athletes in twenty-one sports at the Beijing Olympics. They studied 188 hugs between athletes (both winners and losers) and their coaches, team-mates and rivals.

Hugging has become a national pastime in Britain where it's now pretty well the standard greeting and goodbye between women. And men are at it, too, noisily clapping each other on the back in a blokeish way. You can even do it before you've been properly introduced.

There's a hug for all occasions – for celebration, as in the hurrah-I've-just-got-a-GCSE hug, and for consolation, as in the oh-dear-Tesco-have-sold-out-of-blueberry-muffins-but-never-mind hug. Then there's the Celebrity Hug for people who have been humiliatingly knocked out in the first round of a TV talent show.

When in doubt, hug. And if each one lasts only three seconds, an awful lot of people must be clocking up eight minutes' worth in a single day.

I actually think that it should be an Olympic event – or indeed several Olympic events, with points awarded for artistic impression and also for technique, with the judges paying special attention to the execution of the good clean grasp-and-release manoeuvre. Britain would walk away with the gold medals.

Events would include the Women's Consoling Embrace with Clockwise Back Rub and Multiple Gentle Pats and also the Triathlon, in which the participants first have to sprint 80 metres towards each other and then combine the embrace with an air kiss. There would be team events as well, such as the Mixed Group Hug.

And, of course, the Marathon Hug, over a gruelling five seconds.

I can only see one problem in all this. How will the successful huggers celebrate their victories? I suppose a firm handshake is out of the question.

Omnishambles

I see that politicians have started using the word 'omnishambles' to describe the government's current troubles; they have borrowed it from that satirical TV programme *The Thick of It*. Marketing people also like to make up composite words; 'likeonomics' was one I came across recently. So I thought it would be a good idea to coin some words to describe the difficulties of everyday life.

Fatastrophe. Your new diet was going really well until you accidentally ate a doughnut. Not to be confused with **Chatastrophe**, when you make a horribly inappropriate remark in conversation with someone at a party.

Debarkle. Your dog has an unfortunate encounter with three others in the park.

Fiascolour. That shade of blue looked great on the colour chart, but it's awful now it's on the wall of your living room.

Come a stropper. When you lose your temper and then discover you were in the wrong all the time.

Chaostrich. A mother who puts her head in the sand and carries on sipping her coffee, chatting to a friend or texting while her children run amok in Starbucks.

Prayhem. The Family Service in church is disrupted by younger members of the congregation.

Rucksackus. An altercation with a tourist with a giant rucksack on a crowded train, as he swipes people in the face every time he turns round.

Chavoc. Ugly scenes outside a dodgy nightclub late on Saturday night.

Vodaphobia. This is the feeling you experience when somebody is having a loud and banal conversation on his or her mobile in your vicinity. This is close to **Appoplexy** which is what you experience after a friend has spent twenty-five minutes showing you all the clever things his iPhone can do.

Fizzaster. The result of drinking too many glasses of champagne at your best friend's wedding. This can lead to a **Kisshap** when, to your horror, you find yourself smooching with the wrong person.

Passenger Skill

I have always thought that people should be made to take a test before they are allowed to be front-seat passengers in cars. After a lifetime as a non-driver I have come to realise that sitting beside the person at the wheel requires much more skill than actually driving the car. My opinion has been reinforced by a recent report which showed that motorists take their eyes off the road for 10 per cent of the time they are driving. (Possible distractions include eating, reaching for the phone and text messaging.)

Clearly, it's the duty of the passenger to keep the driver awake, but also to ensure he concentrates on what he is doing. This requires subtlety. The driver believes he is in charge, so he must be gently 'steered' towards making a better job of it.

Passengers must avoid startling revelations, which make the driver turn sharply to look at them. So don't suddenly announce: 'I'm getting a divorce,' or 'I'm on the run from the police.'

Other remarks to avoid include: 'Look at that kestrel hovering over the hard shoulder. Or would you say it's a goshawk? Or could it be a merlin?' Never say, 'Would you like to see my appendix scar?' or 'I've dropped my kebab – can you see it anywhere?'

Try to steal the driver's mobile phone before the start of the journey. Otherwise make sure you are the one doing all the texting. Read the more amusing texts and tweets aloud, to keep him entertained.

Remember that all drivers are touchy and paranoid. They will swerve if you pointedly read out the road sign which says 'Upper Slithering Welcomes Careful Drivers'. Remain calm at all times. Never say: 'Phew! That was a close one', and if you are in charge of putting in the CDs, avoid the sort of music that encourages a lot of vigorous head wagging and banging on the steering wheel.

Postcards

It is reassuring to hear that, even in this age of text and email and Facebook, the good old-fashioned postcard is still holding its own. A survey by *Lonely Planet Traveller*, questioning lots of people, reveals that we still like to put ballpoint to card when we are abroad, even though we have set off fully equipped with smartphones, laptops and other electronic paraphernalia. Even when we are geared up with all the technology, we will still go to the trouble of seeking out the *tabac* where some grumpy shopkeeper may grudgingly agree to sell us a stamp.

My theory is that, while the postcards keep coming, the message has changed. It used to be 'weather v. hot', or 'locals friendly', or 'wonderful little bistro', or 'getting a lovely tan', plus, of course, a lot of glorious sunsets, but now we get a whole new type of news.

Our friends write from the chic French resort of Mauvais-les-Bains that they have found a wonderful little internet café off the beaten track, which, happily, is not overrun by tourists. They no longer boast about how many miles of motorway they clocked up in a day, but how many megabytes they downloaded.

Here are some other friends who are holidaying on the charming Greek island of Myopia. They have sent a picture of the ruined mountain-top monastery of St Apoplexia and the message says, 'It's an exhausting two-hour slog up the mountain to reach this place, but once you get here you are rewarded with a brilliant mobile phone signal.'

And the reported holiday calamities are different. Once upon a time we would get breathless accounts of how Sophie lost Hugo in the warren of steep cobbled streets of the Italian hilltop town, but now Sophie writes about 'two hours of sheer gut-wrenching panic' when she thought she had left the mobile charger at home. In the old days, Sophie would tell us that Hugo was unwell because he had eaten a dodgy octopus or had two of three glasses of the potent local liqueur made of fermented sheep droppings. Now she writes: 'Up all night with the Kindle which was on the blink. Seems to be improving slowly now. Phew!'

And here's a message from our friends Geoff and Peggy in Croatia: 'We've just been on a boat trip and met a very nice couple from Andover. It turns out they have the very same internet service provider as us. Small world!'

Price Labels

At this late stage, I have decided on a major career change. I plan to retrain as the person who turns over those tiny price labels in antique shops and jewellers' windows, so the customer can't see what anything costs. It's a fiddly task, requiring good hand-eye co-ordination, but I have had extensive practice, picking up fluff from the carpet and fitting minuscule circular batteries in the clocks in our house.

After an apprenticeship in label-turning, I expect to be given the added responsibility of writing those meaningless code numbers on the price tags. You know what I mean: you think you see there is actually a price on the pearl earrings, but when you take a closer squint, you find the label says GW76000451. (A lot of husbands and boyfriends will be having this experience as Christmas approaches.)

It's all a marketing ploy, of course, designed to engender the right degree of unease in the customer. By the time the salesperson has located the keys to the cabinets, laboriously found the right key and brought out the bauble, you are a nervous wreck; actual price has lost all meaning and you pay up blindly.

Antique shops take the unease ploy a stage further. There's that unique unsettling smell in the place, which comes from a special antiques trade aerosol spray. It subtly combines the odour of old man's overcoat, mouldy leather, attic dust and tired lavender. This creates just the right amount of dizziness in the customer. They also distribute special unstable objects round the shop, so you are in constant dread of an awful accident.

Interesting items are displayed low down in the cabinets, so you have to squat and twist your head round awkwardly in an effort to make out the price on the label. You become giddy and topple over, crashing into the nearby Georgian tea set which probably costs as much as GW76000451.

Seating Arrangement

Boy, girl, boy, girl, boy, girl, boy, boy . . . Oh dear, that won't work. Don't sit down yet, we can get this right. Remember that army general sounding off the other week about how husbands and wives shouldn't sit next to each other at formal dinners? He has certainly complicated

our lovely family get-together today. It's like going on manoeuvres.

Right, let's start again with Grandpa. He's a little deaf in his left ear and needs to be near the loo. So if Grandpa sits there and we go girl, boy, girl, boy . . . No, stand up again everyone, that will only work if Tom and Helen agree to get divorced and Eric is declared an honorary girl.

I've got it. You all stay exactly where you are and I'll go and sit at the other end of the restaurant at a table for one. I can wave to you. No, that won't do; Aunt Jean and Aunt Susan haven't spoken for seven years, so have to be farther apart.

Let's get this done. The waiter is sighing and the people at the next table are scowling because we are looming over them and blocking out their light. Poor Grandpa has changed places four times and urgently needs to sit down. No, we can't disinvite Aunt Susan. She's family. Did the general mention if living together counted as being married? I don't think he would approve.

I've got it. If we borrow a woman from the people at the scowling table and she sits next to Grandpa on his deaf side, the problem is solved. Eureka! Alternatively, Eric could go and join them. If he sat next to the angry-looking woman in blue, it would also sort out their boy-girl thing very nicely. I'll just go and ask them.

No, they're not keen. Oh dear, we should have invited Grandpa's ex-wife after all. Never mind, there's a solution. Waiter, do you do takeaways?

Small Print

I'm afraid I'm a bit behind with my reading. A booklet arrived from the bank several weeks ago, spelling out some revisions to its terms and conditions, and I'm supposed to study it carefully and keep it in a safe place. Unfortunately, I've forgotten where that safe place is. Anyway, I can't tackle the bank's communication until I've read the Important Safety Notes, which came with the alarm clock radio and which I was commanded to read FIRST.

I dread parties in case somebody asks me: 'Have you read the leaflet that comes with those blood pressure tablets?' I'll stare at my feet and mumble: 'No, but I hear it's very good.' Then they'll say: 'Everybody's talking about it. The list of possible side effects is a *tour de force*.'

It's the same with my online reading. When I buy something I click on the 'Accept' button and pretend

I'm aware of all the reams of terms and conditions, just praying that a team of hard-faced men from the Internet Examination Board doesn't show up on my doorstep to test my knowledge.

It's a pity you can't get a synopsis of the small print. Even better, there should be critics, so we could simply read the reviews. 'I found the conditions printed on the train ticket to Andover somewhat derivative. We've read much the same thing before on numerous day returns.' Or: 'There were some good twists in the plot in the safety notes, but I wasn't convinced that anyone would leave a clock radio out in the rain. It lacked the poignant imagery you find in those warnings about children under five swallowing the smaller components of electric toothbrushes.'

Or finally: 'This is another great page-turner from NatWest. I was on the edge of my seat right up to the *denouement*. I mustn't give the end away, but something shattering happens to Clause 44b(ix).'

Sorry

I'm sorry but that is just plain wrong. The New York Bakery Co, in some research which is probably just an unapologetic attempt to get some publicity, claims the British say 'sorry' eight times a day. It's far more often than that. Think of the number of times a day you nearly bump into somebody, or you need to interrupt somebody (it has replaced 'Ahem') and, most of all in this noisy world, you didn't quite catch what was said. 'Sorry' is one of those auto-pilot words or phrases we use to get us through the day.

'Lovely' is another one. 'How were your starters?' the waitress asks. 'Lovely,' you reply automatically. 'Lovely,' she says. 'Sorry,' she says as she prepares to put the next course on the table. 'Sorry,' you reply, as you move the side plate out of the way. You can be certain that she will soon be back to ask 'How were your mains?' After that, she will want to know, 'How was everything?' Yes, it was all lovely.

You go into a shop and the assistant says, 'Are you all right there?' (This has replaced 'Can I help you?') You make your purchase and the assistant tells you how much that comes to. 'Lovely,' you say, handing over the money. 'Lovely,' he says, putting it in the till. 'Lovely,' he adds, giving you your change. 'Lovely,' you say, taking it. 'Take care,' he says as you leave.

We were staying in a hotel for a few days last week and whenever we made the slightest request to the staff the answer was always 'No problem at all'. It slowly drove me mad. I told myself that next time one of them said it I would trip them up. Then I would say, 'Sorry.' Or perhaps, 'Lovely.' Or maybe, 'Are you all right there?'

Anyway, enjoy the rest of your day.

Useless

The fondue set has just come out top in a survey of useless gadgets that clutter up our kitchen cupboards. The soda maker comes second, closely followed by the utterly dispensable melon baller. This is a wonderful survey to conduct, a fascinating picture of all our follies, illusions and past high hopes.

When I fumble through the second drawer in our kitchen unit, making a noise like a bicycle thrown down three flights of stairs, I find all sorts of things that seemed like a good idea at the time. There's a potato ricer, for goodness' sake, wooden and metal skewers for brochettes we've never made, mortars without matching pestles and

pestles without mortars, a stone for sharpening carving knives and half a dozen carving knives I have success-fully blunted, and nine bottle openers, betraying my deep-seated fear of being without a bottle opener. Also several tin openers that never lived up to expectations, and some once-used whisks and pastry brushes.

The fondue set must surely soon achieve the status of being a historic object. Somebody will take one to the *Antiques Roadshow*. 'It was handed down to me by my granny,' the owner will say. 'I've no idea what it's for, but I'm told that she used to keep her melon ballers in it.'

Most gadgets are toys which we fondly believe will make a dull job somehow fun. The trouble is, once you have had the fun using the gadget you still have the dull job of cleaning it, poking out the little holes in the garlic press, dismantling the juicer or whatever.

In my experience, the dullest job of all is flossing. I have a vast collection of devices to make it more interesting – battery-operated flossers, dinky little brushes, prodders, objects shaped like longbows and miniature harps. One day I'll take them all to the *Antiques Roadshow*. Fiona Bruce will be impressed.

Wimbledon

I believe I am better prepared for Wimbledon this year than ever before. I've been working hard, practising how to pronounce the name of the Moldovan player with the huge serve and I'm pretty sure I can now distinguish him from the Slovenian who is master of the heavy back-spin lob. I've also been putting in a lot of hours, polishing my knowledge of ligaments, tendons, Achilles heels, thigh strains and troublesome groins.

The game of watching tennis on TV has changed immeasurably over recent years. Nowadays the viewer brings at least three remote controls onto the sofa for any match. Of course, the remote controls themselves are now lightweight and much more streamlined and powerful than they were in the old days.

We also have to master the interactive game and I must say I'm very happy with my red button thumb technique, so that I can quickly switch away from the plucky English girl who is having a torrid time on an outside court and, with lightning reflexes, I can press the blue button to avoid Sue Barker's interminable interview with a dull expert who got knocked out in the second round sometime in the 1980s. Yes, my game has come on in leaps and bounds since the days when I didn't know

which one was Venus and which one was Serena.

My wife and I have been working very hard on our doubles game. After every point we have to walk to each other across the sitting room and briefly touch hands. This is much harder than it looks and if you don't get your timing just right you can find yourself flapping at thin air. Often we discuss tactics, putting our hands in front of our mouths so that nobody can lip-read. Then my wife will whisper: 'Shall we see if there is anything more interesting happening on Court Two?'

Wish

Make a wish. Somebody is bound to issue that dreaded command when you successfully pull a wishbone, take your first bite of a mince pie or blow out the birthday candles. This is a real poser. Your mind goes blank, but you feel you can't miss this opportunity, or the people in the mince pie wish-fulfilment department will give up on you, or the wishbone authorities will despair. You can't really wish for World Peace, because you did that last time and look where it got us all. You could always go for the 'good health' option, but it has become a bit of a cliché. You could try wishing for 'immense wealth', but this usually leads to a misunderstanding resulting in a £10 Lottery win five months later.

At least you should be grateful you are not being visited by a Good Fairy offering *three* wishes, putting a real strain on your powers of imagination and making you wish you could snap her wand in two pieces.

I suppose the answer is to prepare your wish in advance and make it specific and low maintenance – like, for example, 'I wish for some brandy butter to go with this mince pie', or 'I wish that we have duck next time because it doesn't have a wishbone.' Maybe there is somebody present who is in need of some improvement; you could always wish for them to be made a better person. Next time I find myself in this sort of situation, I'm going to ask for a rain check, to let me use my wish in a month's time when I may have a more pressing need.

I had an aunt who always made the same wish. She would prissily announce, 'I wished for everything to be nice.' This so enraged the rest of the family that they would beat her about the head with their crackers.

Fibs

Have you, really, read *Crime and Punishment?* Apparently, it's one of the Top 10 Books We Say We Have Read But Haven't. So are *To Kill a Mockingbird* and *A Passage to India*. This research started me thinking about other questions whose answer is likely to be a fib. Here are twenty-four, but not necessarily the Top 24:

- Do you floss?
- After this delicious Sunday lunch some of us are going for a good brisk walk across the ploughed field in the rain. Would you like to join us?

- Now be frank, do you really think this colour suits me?

- It's a new recipe I've been trying out. Can you taste the dill?

- How many sit-ups did you do?

- Have you heard the one about this horse which goes into a bar . . . ?

- Wow! Do you see the nuthatch in that bush over there?

- Do you mind if we join you?

- Timmy isn't bothering you, is he?

- Are you warm enough?

- Don't you just love charades?

- Would you like to see my stamp collection/new shed/operation scar/hilarious thing on YouTube?

- Would you agree that the tannins in this wine are just right?

- Are you comfortable sitting on the floor?

- Mummy, what have you done with that picture I brought home from school specially for you?

- Tell me honestly, don't you agree that my fiancé Gerald is the most wonderful person in the whole wide world?

- I'm a vegan. Is that going to be a terrible nuisance?

- Oh, I'm so sorry. How awfully clumsy of me. Did I hurt you?

- Have you read our Terms and Conditions?

- Will we be seeing you in church next Sunday?

- Are these leeks from your own garden?

- Do you think the new baby looks like me?
- Do say if the dog is too much. He is rather large. Are you all right with him on your lap?
- Did you manage to read this article right to the end?

Handshake

Is it time to wave goodbye to the handshake? A survey, telling us what we could easily have guessed, suggests that, as a form of greeting, the hug and the kiss on the cheek are rapidly gaining ground. As many as 42 per cent of those questioned said they would never shake hands when greeting a friend and 8 per cent said it was unhygienic. (Presumably these 8 per cent are, nonetheless, enthusiastic huggers.)

I have written here before that if hugging became an Olympic event Britain would win all the medals, but now I think it is time to launch a Save the Handshake campaign. It was once a natural reflex to shake hands with someone when introduced, but now we are just as likely to give a vague wave, say 'hiya', and immediately forget their name. Male friends (of a certain age) greet each other with a handshake, but it's often ironical, a sort of mock formality.

Oddly enough, I realised last week that, whenever I go to my dentist, we shake hands; maybe, as with boxers, it's supposed to convey a 'no hard feelings' message. The only other person who tried to shake my hand last week was a charity mugger in the street, trying to ensnare me into listening to his spiel.

So, to kick off my campaign, I suggest we all resolve to shake hands with someone at least once day. That's just for a start. Let us offer the proper hand of friendship. This might do something to combat that tiresome hand-touching habit which has become such a major interruption in sport. Later this month, at the Wimbledon championships, doubles partners will waste so much energy walking all the way across the court just to touch hands after every point, after every ace and even after every damn double fault. It makes me so mad I want to shake my fist at them.

Home Life

Birth Certificate

Congratulations to President Obama for producing his birth certificate to confound all those conspiracy theorists who have been claiming that he was not born in the United States. I mean, of course, congratulations to him for *finding* his birth certificate.

I imagine that all business at the White House was suspended for two days while the President hunted for this pesky document and his wife Michelle made helpful suggestions. 'Mr President, honey,' she probably said, 'have you looked in that special envelope where you keep the secret code for unleashing nuclear war? Or maybe it's in that box where you put last year's Christmas card from the Clintons.' I'm guessing his Chief of Staff managed to produce the key to the locked drawer of the desk in the Oval Office, but all they found inside was a note of

Angela Merkel's new mobile phone number, the card of a Washington mini-cab firm and a certificate to show that the Obama family dog Bo had had all the necessary vaccinations.

Birth certificates seem somehow to be able to escape from filing cabinets. You open a folder marked Very Important Things and all you find is a certificate showing that you passed a few A levels many years ago. The trouble with birth certificates is that they tend to be put in that fatal place we call 'somewhere safe'. Other items in the same conspiracy to escape to the Land of the Lost Dry Cleaning Ticket include the Allen key, which you only succeed in locating when you are hunting for the key for bleeding radiators – and vice versa, of course. You also have a fine collection of expired guarantees – for long-abandoned electrical equipment, but nothing for the new blender which has started acting weirdly. If President Obama's opponents want to catch him out now, maybe they should call on him to produce his library ticket.

Missing Workmen

We have all heard of Empty Nest Syndrome when children finally leave home and parents feel lost, listless and cast down, but a related affliction, known as Vacant Stepladder Blues, is less well known. This occurs when builders or decorators at last finish the job and move out of your house.

You never thought you would miss them, but you discover you feel a little pang when you walk into a room and find there is nobody there sanding the wall or knocking it down, or leaning on it. There is not even a radio playing raucous music loudly to itself. You look out of the window and all you see is the view where there used to be feet on a ladder.

Without realising it, you got to know those men; you recognised the different ringtones of their mobile phones. Poignant reminders of their stay have been left behind – an encrusted paintbrush, a hammer, a pair of scuffed shoes, a tattered sweater on a peg behind the door.

There's a coffee mug on the doorstep. You recognise it, you know which one of the builders always had that one and you find yourself murmuring: 'Milky coffee, one and a half sugars.' Their presence meant you always had to keep up certain standards. While they were here you always dressed for breakfast, closed the door when you went to the bathroom and made sure you never ran out of chocolate Hobnobs.

In a way they were just like your older children. They would go missing for a day or two with no explanation; you would find yourself looking out of the window to see if they were coming down the road. Perhaps one day they'll pick up that sweater.

At the moment, we have decorators painting the outside of the house where we live. I keep telling myself not to get too fond of them.

Car Alarm

It's good to observe the changing seasons in the city. Now we are witnessing the first stirrings of the summer car alarms. It may be the hot weather or perhaps just a fat moth landing on the bonnet that causes it, but it seems they always go off on Sunday morning at 4.17 by the bedside digital clock.

It lasts for four minutes, then stops abruptly, raising false hopes, then starts again. I lie in bed composing sarcastic letters to leave on the windscreen. 'Dear Renault Owner, Thank you very much for completely ruining . . .' I begin. I wonder if I should address it curtly by its licence plate number, second half only, as if it were the surname. 'XMV: it may interest you to know that while you were snoozing in your dinky weekend country cottage, some of us . . .' The on-street parking round here is so dire that the owner of the car which is mooing out there is probably fast asleep two streets away. This calls for a more brutal note: 'Get back to Fairfield Road where you belong!' (Plus optional skull and crossbones.)

It's now 4.47 a.m. and, as the two-note wail goes on, I polish my prose. I wonder if Renault owners 'get' sarcasm and if the jibe about weekend cottages could be sharpened. I will go out there to check the licence plate number. Then I'll lean against the side of some other car to make an adjustment to my stinging letter. This will set off that car alarm, a porch light will come on and I'll be discovered with my masterpiece of invective still in my hand.

As I lie in bed going through these scenarios I suddenly notice the car alarm has stopped. The peace is startling. By now I am thoroughly wound up and I start to compose another letter: 'Dear Eerie Silence, I suppose you think it's clever . . .'

Census

The Census form is on top of our fridge. This is good. It means that it has now entered the carefully worked out filing system I use for such things as Income Tax returns, reminders from the dentist and new Terms and Conditions notices from the bank. The fridge is useful for keeping milk fresh, but its main function is to be my Pending Tray.

Soon the Census form will get promotion to the front left-hand corner of my desk. This is for matters needing urgent attention. After a few days, when it is half-buried under letters and leaflets, I will make the executive decision to transfer it to my sock drawer. This move signifies 'Action This Day'. Every time I get a clean pair of socks the Census form will be lying in wait for me; the sickly purple markings on the envelope will be a reproach.

A document normally stays here five days and then I move it to the chair in the bedroom. The Census form is now in a Code Red situation. I see it last thing at night and the idea is that it will disturb my dreams. Members of the Office for National Statistics, all dressed in purple, will swirl about the bed, pointing accusing fingers, and I will leap up in terror at 3 a.m. and fill in the form.

If that doesn't work, it's officially an emergency and I will write 'Census' on a slip of paper and put it in my right-hand trouser pocket so I find it every time I reach for my keys. Three days later I'll get another slip of paper, write 'Census' in block capitals and put it in my left-hand trouser pocket. This should do the trick. I'll now be ready to fill in the form when I've found a pen. There should be one on top of the fridge.

Cold Callers

Yes, I know they can be a pest and an intrusion, but I'm beginning to feel the teeniest bit of sympathy for cold callers. Nobody likes those chummy chaps who ring us up for 'just a quick one, if I may', about supplying all our energy needs, or a service agreement covering our gutters, or great news of a special offer on fitted kitchens. They give themselves away immediately by asking after your health. 'How are you today?' they wonder, and the answer is that you are on your guard.

Nowadays you hear many stories about how people deal with these intrusions. They keep the cold caller hanging on, they pretend to be a child or the Mexican butler or a religious fanatic; they order a takeaway or sing the Norwegian national anthem or offer to phone back.

The cold caller must know all about these ploys; he's heard them a dozen times before. He knows he's the object of scorn, but he needs the job. He must remain polite in the face of all this contumely. That's why I have to sympathise with him. I just hope there is a place where cold callers can go and meet each other and exchange stories about their experiences at work and compare the number of times they've been hung up on; somewhere they can respect each other as fellow Telephonic Outreach Consultants.

Let's hope it is a cheery bar, named the Dialling Tone, perhaps, where they gather at the end of the day and clap each other on the back. 'How are you today? That's excellent,' they say. 'Just a quick one about a special offer of a pint of beer. As a valued fellow Telephonic Outreach Consultant, you now qualify for a bonus packet of crisps with that beer and, if I may, I'd like to take some time to tell you my latest funny story. Cheers.'

Hiding

Apparently, the sock drawer is the most popular place to hide valuables. About 13 per cent of us choose it. After that, we put our heirlooms under the bed – where, presumably, the burglar is already lying, just waiting for them to be handed to him.

Valuables in the sock drawer? What nonsense. The sock drawer is the place for broken sunglasses, a magnifying glass, old alarm clocks, a scattering of toothpicks and a tattered school photograph – plus a sock or three. Putting your valuables in your sock drawer is also a bit of a cliché, like hiding the door key under the mat.

I spend a lot of time watching crime thrillers to get ideas. Not ideas to commit the perfect murder, but for new hiding places. My favourite moment is when the glamorous woman cop stands at the door holding up a piece of paper and says: 'I have a warrant to search this place.' Now I'm agog to see where her officers will look. In the earth under the potted plant perhaps, or up the chimney. They rip open the mattress, but that's too obvious and there's nothing there.

They usually tip out all the cereal packets and I immediately wonder about hiding my secret wad of cash in the bran flakes, but then I'm afraid the burglar may have seen the same film.

I need to find a clever place, but the trouble is, if it's too clever, I will outwit myself. If I put a slip of paper with my PIN number in the teapot, I may have to leave myself a note saying 'PIN number in teapot'. I must then remember that I put this note inside a book called *A History of Banking.*

That's the trouble with hiding valuables. We forget and they're lost. It would be so nice just to call a glamorous woman cop to come round with a search warrant.

Recorded

It makes me proud to think I have made a major contribution to education and, long after I've gone, teachers will refer to me as 'a resource'. I have made so many thousands of phone calls that were almost certainly recorded for training purposes, so somewhere there is a priceless archive with yard after yard of catalogued and neatly labelled recordings of my conversations with councils, energy companies, train operators, stores and call centres.

I picture classrooms full of eager young men and women looking forward to careers in the exciting world of helpdesks and customer relations, hanging on every word of the tutor with a PhD in Telephonic Client-Management Skills. The tutor opens her (or his) briefcase and, with a flourish, produces a cassette of some call I made in the past. It is a classic case-study.

'Did you observe,' the tutor says, 'how the caller launched into his saga of previously unavailing calls and how the operative allowed him to continue at some length, then interrupted and asked him his postcode and the first line of his address? This is what I would call the perfect ploy for wrong-footing the caller.'

The students scribble notes furiously as the tutor continues. 'In the next tape I am going to play you, the same customer starts off by giving his postcode, expecting he will now have a free run with his tale of woe, but you see our wily operative cuts in and asks him for his nine-digit customer number. Never forget, the customer reference number is your best weapon.'

The tutor plays more of my tapes, showing how to lose a call by transferring it to another department and demonstrating the pitch-perfect way of saying, 'Is there anything else I can help you with today?'

And when the lecture is over the students linger to replay my greatest hits while they take a break over coffee, biscuits and some Vivaldi.

Sleep

It's not considered admirable to sleep well. The phrase 'like a log' sums it up, suggesting that the good sleeper is merely a mindless, useless lump of wood. So people don't admit to it; when asked how their night was, they say 'troubled' or claim they 'couldn't get off' or they slept 'fitfully'. I suppose it's a sort of Henry IV complex – uneasy lies the head that wears a crown.

The only time we say we slept well is when we spend the night in somebody else's house or maybe in a hotel. Then we overdo it. In reply to the question at breakfast time, we say: 'Never better. It was absolutely amazing. Must be the air round here. That mattress is fantastic.' All polite lies. In fact it was too dark or too light, the mattress sloped, the building creaked, a dog barked and you didn't dare go to the loo.

My life was changed the other day when I read a report of a study which said that sour cherry juice before bed boosts the level of the hormone melatonin and adds an extra twenty-five minutes sleep a night. The really exciting bit was that it said this increases 'sleep efficiency' by up to 6 per cent. Suddenly there is no stigma attached to my snooze and my zizz is guilt-free. So now I don't sleep like a log, I have a very efficient night's sleep and I put in a very workmanlike eight hours.

My wife, on the other hand, is an incompetent sleeper. I'm sorry to say she is just not proficient; her productivity is low and she lacks the necessary sleep skills. For the first time I find myself on the moral high ground in the morning. When asked how my night was, I say, 'It was very businesslike, actually. In fact I slept like a time and motion manager.'

Washing Up

Those of you who own dishwashers may like to know that the rest of us who are still chained to the kitchen sink are having enormous fun. In the days when you last wielded a washing-up sponge you probably just had a choice of two types of detergent – Original or Lemon Scented. It's a whole new world of foam these days. I am currently soaping the dinner plates with Grapefruit and Bergamot. With added moisturisers, it goes without saying. These detergents are not just kind to your hands, they're falling over themselves to please.

So, this week it's Grapefruit and Bergamot for me; next time I might decide to dabble in Pomegranate and Honeysuckle or Blackberry and Rosemary or I might go mad and try Cucumber and Basil. There's also Aloe Vera and Cucumber, but I might get that confused with my aloe vera shampoo.

I suppose all these flavours are dreamed up in the detergent laboratories to relieve us of some of the boredom of washing up. Even a decent tea towel is a distraction. That's why, to entertain us, they are printed with a guide to the more obscure herbs, or samples of Yorkshire dialect, naval distress signals or a London Underground map. Put your soapy hand up if you, too, have a tea towel covered with childish portraits of the pupils at your local primary school.

So, as I scrape the encrusted mustard off the plate I can mutter pithy Yorkshire sayings, plan Tube journeys and dream of the exotic aromas on offer on the supermarket shelves. They sound almost like desserts in a fancy restaurant – dainty jellies, perhaps, of Lavender and Mandarin, or Almond, or Tangerine and Ginger Blossom. Or, I've just realised, they could be bubble baths. Are people climbing into a foaming Pomegranate and Honeysuckle bath with a heap of dirty dishes? Have I been missing something here?

Whistle

What happened to whistling? It has been suggested that the habit seems to have died out. These days, chaps sauntering in the street are more likely to be on their phones or listening to iPods. Last week I discovered one place, at least, where whistling survives: in a men's changing room. I went for a swim for the first time in yonks and there, as they dressed and undressed, the males were all emitting that good old-fashioned tuneless noise.

I suppose it was meant to be a sign of nonchalance as they stripped in the presence of strangers, and also, perhaps a sort of warning signal – 'Look out, I've got a bare bottom and I'm about to appear suddenly round the corner at the end of the lockers.' Or: 'Attention! Soapy nude emerging from shower.'

It's also a warning signal used by window cleaners. They whistle while they wipe, as a way of telling us where they are in the house or which window ledge they are on. It's also to reassure us, to suggest they couldn't whistle while simultaneously pocketing our jewels or reading our private correspondence. I guess the window cleaner also wants to give an impression of nonchalance. His whistling says:

'You may feel a bit uncomfortable having me wandering round your house with my bucket, but actually I feel perfectly at home.'

Men, doing something technical, which needs concentration, like rewiring a plug or unscrewing a tiny screw, also whistle. This, again, is a warning signal. It says: 'This is much more tricky than you realise. Don't say anything to distract me.'

A man who whistles – and surely it's nearly always a man – is telling people he is quite content in his own company. That's why it's tuneless. If he produced a recognisable melody, some stranger might come along and join in and make it a duet. What an intrusion that would be.

Slob

A lot of hard work goes into relaxing. You'd think it would be a simple process for most people, but there are thousands of experts just bursting to teach us relaxation techniques or to show us how to achieve deep relaxation. This gives me an idea. I happen to believe that

it is beneficial, from time to time and in the privacy of your own home, to be a slob.

How about a course teaching people to be slobs? There would be master classes in slob techniques and workshops helping clients to achieve a state of deep slobdom. Join us for a session of synchronised yawning and scratching, followed by lessons in the correct posture when sitting in a chair with your legs dangling over the arms. Let our tutors demonstrate the art of using your fingers to comb your hair and then attend a lecture on the Theory and Practice of the Rotation of Dirty Socks.

Pupils attending the three-day course will be issued with their own personalised pre-scruffed bathrobe which they will wear for the duration. Breakfast will be taken standing up, leaning over the kitchen pedal bin, and will consist of crumbs from last night's crisp packet poured straight down the throat, plus a lick inside an empty yoghurt pot.

For lunch, also standing up, you will be taught the correct way to hold a whole slice of bread, without letting the honey run off it, while opening a carton of orange juice with your teeth. Dinner is a more formal affair – a pick and mix buffet at the open fridge. After dinner there will be a contest to see who is best at closing the fridge door using only their hip.

Those who successfully complete the course will attend a graduation ceremony where they will be handed a smudged diploma, which they will then toss in the general direction of the wastepaper basket.

Late Life

Armchair

Like most men, I suppose, I regard my armchair as My Territory. I defend it fiercely against invading backsides and I wouldn't dream of parking myself anywhere else in the living room. You would probably call the colour plum red, though the plums would be over-ripe ones that had been knocked about a bit. The three cushions on it have been beaten into submission and when I lean back on them they are scrunched up the way I like them.

The arms of the chair are broad and just right for thumping when I want to express a strong opinion or protest at something on the TV. Over the years the seat has become strangely lopsided. It slopes to the left as if I slump in an odd position or perhaps one half of my body is heavier than the other. Sometimes I try to correct this lopsidedness by leaning far to the right, as if I was on a sailing boat in a high wind. It doesn't work.

Next to my armchair there is a daffodil-yellow three-legged stool where I put my coffee mug. It was painted that colour so long ago that I can't remember who should take the blame. Seated in my armchair and looking round the room, I see that the furniture here is a random accumulation, but if an interior designer happened to walk in, I would tell him it was an eclectic mix or a witty combination, part of my overall concept.

I would explain to him that my armchair sloped because I'd sent it to an exclusive furniture distorter with a workshop in the Cotswolds and it was intended to harmonise with the gentle slope in the floorboards. (I might also hint that this flat is actually our second home and that we spend most of our time in a stylishly converted gasholder in the fashionable end of Basingstoke.)

I'd indicate some quirky touches, pointing to the mantelpiece where we have our *objet trouvé* – an important-looking brass screw I found on the floor which must have come off something or other and must be absolutely vital. I'd also draw attention to our *object perdu* – the decorative knob which is missing from one end of the curtain rail. It is a pleasing point of focus in the room.

Oh yes, from where I sit, leaning somewhat to the left, the overall picture is perfect.

Barber

What is the name of the place a man goes to for a haircut? Of course, there is the old distinction between a barber and a hairdresser, but now there are so many more nuances. Within easy walking distance of where I live I have a choice of Franco's His & Hers, Capelli's Gentlemen's Grooming, a Hair Studio, two shiny establishments which call themselves Hair Cutters and two Barbers. And there's even a subtle difference between the barbers. One is a Gentlemen's Barber, but I go to the other one, which is called a Gents Salon. There's something a bit jaunty about that name; it makes you feel you are on the way to the races.

The words 'Hair Studio' and 'Hair Cutters' tell you all you need to know. These are places where they have check-in desks and where you tip your head backwards over the basin when you have a shampoo. That is too much swank for my thinning hair, which doesn't like a fuss and doesn't want undue attention drawn to it.

'A tidy-up, sir?' my kindly barber asks, knowing that I just want to be made to look a little less like a mad professor from a dodgy university. Some people are dead against conversation while they have their hair cut, but I don't mind at all, so long as the man with the scissors

doesn't mention Arsenal and doesn't say, 'Keeping busy?'

Having removed my glasses I sit in front of the blurred stranger in the mirror opposite and have a restful conversation with my barber. Whenever I express a mild opinion or make a bland observation, he leaps upon it and claims it. 'This is it!' he says. 'This is what I'm saying.' Then he deftly snips the tufts in my ears.

Then, when it is nearly finished, he leans over and murmurs confidentially. These days it's not, 'Something for the weekend, sir?' It's, 'A little bit off the eyebrows?'

Selling Flat

We are in the process of selling our flat. And what a process it is, filling in those forms and hunting down all the documents the seller is required to provide. I've been lifting up the carpet to see if any Japanese knotweed is lurking underneath, staring out of the window wondering where my boundaries are and whether any of my pipes and wires cross a neighbour's property.

Some of the questions are so weird or so irrelevant that you get the feeling you are being tested by some know-all clever Dick whose aim in life is to catch you out. You feel like a young American Indian brave hoping to be

initiated in the Navajo tribe. You stand before the elders and they say: 'You've slain a bear with your bare hands, you've managed to swim across a raging torrent and you have climbed a sheer mountain. That's all very well, but now can you provide us with a BS7671 Electrical Safety Certificate?'

Now I'm scrabbling through chaotic files, just in case I might find a Tree Preservation Order or the results of a test for radon gas, or a certificate from a builder, and I am wondering if a receipt for the supply of a loose cover for an armchair and the phone number of a reliable minicab firm might do instead. It's clear to me that the ideal property advertisement would read: 'Superb filing system for sale – with rather nice flat thrown in free of charge.'

As soon as I have finished this lot, I will have to move on to the Fittings and Contents Form. This contains some thorny philosophical questions. Do we intend to leave behind the water butt and the rotary clothes line we do not have? And, by the way, what kind of people, leaving their old home behind, would feel a compulsion to take their toilet-roll holder with them?

Dinner Jacket

Reluctantly, I went to hire a dinner jacket last week. This is not my favourite thing and I certainly did not feel as comfortable as the other customer in the shop, who was nonchalantly hiring five morning suits (for best man and ushers, I suppose) while sending texts on his mobile phone.

I'm stuffy about dinner jackets and I told the assistant I didn't want any fancy-pants stuff. The cream tuxedo is for bounders and card-sharps and the burgundy bow tie with matching cummerbund is for the man who expects to be misbehaving before the night is over. And the pale mauve ruffled shirt-front, like the icing on an exotic cupcake, is best avoided unless you are a dodgy dance-band leader.

No, the look I was going for was 'Odeon cinema manager *circa* 1955', as I made clear to the attentive assistant. (Actually my ideal dinner jacket would be one handed down through four generations of my family and turned greenish and mildewed after all the years in damp and draughty country mansions. Unfortunately, my ancestors didn't oblige.)

The assistant got out his tape measure and, like two geographers arguing about the direction of true north, we got into the discussion about where my waist might be located. Eventually a decision was reached and he produced a jacket and trousers for me to try on.

The jacket was fine but the trousers sagged round my middle and were so long they made a messy pile-up at my ankles. He went away and brought another pair. When I emerged (sheepishly) from the changing cubicle next time, the assistant was delighted. 'I think I've found you, sir,' he said, like an artist who has finally captured the essence of his subject. And I think I've found myself. The main feature starts in five minutes and there are still seats available in the three and nines.

Dry-cleaners

I am being persecuted by the dry-cleaners and abused by the laundry. They bombard me with abusive messages. My trousers come back from the dry-cleaners with labels attached saying: 'The remaining stains on the garment have been examined. We feel that any further attempts to remove them could result in damage to either the colour or the material.' Meanwhile the laundry also uses the rather disdainful word 'garment' to describe my shirt and, in fact, the message is the same. Sometimes they also point out (tersely) that a shirt collar is frayed or a cuff is torn.

I'm the first to admit that I could never be described as a neat person, that I do tend to carry leaky pens in the back pocket of my trousers and I am inclined to hurl the ingredients about with abandon when I'm cooking and can recklessly splosh wine and olive oil, but all the same a chap has feelings, you know. Sometimes I'm afraid the dry-cleaners will reject my garments altogether and suggest that I take my scruffy custom elsewhere as I am lowering the tone of their establishment.

You may wonder why I don't spare myself some of this criticism by getting a washing machine. When I hear about the experiences of other people who have one it

always sounds like they have an extra, rather tyrannical and hypochondriac member of the family, grumbling away for hours in the next room.

I put up with the laundry because it offers a chance of the unexpected. Sometimes it sends me back an interesting pair of socks which is certainly not mine. I wear the socks and return them the next week. Occasionally I get someone else's shirt. It's like being a member of a clothes-sharing club. Maybe, at this moment, some elegant gentleman is getting one of my shirts with a snooty message about stains.

Early

We all know people who are always unfailingly late. They can't help it; it's a disease and we make allowances for them. But what about those of us who are chronically early? I call this affliction pre-punctuality and I believe that those who suffer from it deserve more sympathy. This thought occurred to me last week when I was waiting to catch a plane to Glasgow, glancing at the departures board for the 7,581st time and seeing the same dread message: 'Wait in lounge'.

If I could have back all the hours I've wasted by arriving

too early for planes, trains, appointments and restaurant bookings I could learn Mandarin and train to be an airline pilot and still have hours left over to read Burton's *Anatomy of Melancholy* four times.

That proverb about the early bird is wrong. The sad truth is that the early bird has to hang around for ages, pacing up and down, waiting for the worm to show up. We who suffer from pre-punctuality are often mocked, but we make a vital contribution to society. We drink millions of unnecessary cups of coffee just to fill in time. Starbucks and Costa would collapse without us, but what thanks do we get? We spend so much time mooching in railway stations that we ought to be able to earn Sock Shop miles. Dentists are cheered up, mistaking our pre-punctuality for eagerness.

Sitting under that departures board last week, I decided my epitaph ought to be 'He waited in lounge'. Then I realised that, sometime in the future, I and my fellow sufferers will be standing in a fidgeting huddle outside the Pearly Gates, looking at our watches every two minutes, trying to decide if we can fit in one more espresso, regretting we had been so quick in finishing the Quick Crossword and wondering when the Last Trump will finally sound.

My Cold

My wife has a cold and she says she got it from me. Actually, what she tells friends and anyone who asks is that I 'kindly donated' it to her. The cold may have dulled her sense of smell, but her irony is still intact. If I may be permitted to make a few observations here, I can't see how she can be sure that she has 'my' cold. She is an independent person, she gets around and she has her own sources for germs.

Admittedly, she got it four days after mine started, but that could have been a coincidence. Or, if I may dare to suggest this, perhaps she got her cold, spontaneously, out

of empathy; she identified herself with my suffering and came to experience the same symptoms. That would be a rather beautiful thing.

There is another reason I believe her cold did not come from me. Mine was a truly epic cold. It was, you could say, the Olympic opening ceremony of colds. It had drama, with sensational clusters of sneezes and ear-splitting nose blowing; it had emotion, with tragic coughing fits, a sore throat and a croak; it had spectacle, with gushing eyes. Thousands of tissues were lavished on this production.

Now – and I'm going to put this as kindly as I can – my wife's cold is a pale imitation. The sneezes, nose blowing and coughing just don't have the same oomph. I hope this won't be taken amiss, but she has a cold which is *masquerading* as mine and, in doing so, is damaging the brand. We all seem to want to identify the source of our cold, to explain it, to point the finger and to name the guilty germ carrier, but a terrible mistake has been made in this case.

I'm thinking of copyrighting my cold – and, by the way, it's still not better.

TV Set

I love the month of June and all its summer delights, like Ascot and Trooping the Colour. In our house, the traditional June event takes place in the week of the Queen's Club tennis tournament. It is our Great TV Set Discussion.

My wife declares it open with a short speech, saying : 'Wimbledon is coming up soon; we ought to get a new TV set.'

'This set is fine,' I say. 'It's part of the family.' It was handed down to us by our daughter fifteen years ago.

'We've been watching Wimbledon all these years and we've never actually seen the ball,' my wife replies.

'You mean to say they play tennis with balls?' I say. 'I thought Wimbledon was all about pictures of the spectators and the Royal box and long psychobabble interviews with players saying they are "in a good place right now" and "happy on grass". The ball isn't the point.'

I am very happy with our set. It goes back a long way in every sense – none of that new-fangled flat-screen plasma nonsense. It's also an Extra Low Definition model and, as I tell my wife, if we get a new set the picture will be too good and we'll be distracted by the pores and blemishes of the presenters.

I like to think we are ahead of the trend. Our programmes have been in semi-darkness long before all those Scandinavian and French *noir* thrillers came along. (And not being able to read sub-titles is educational.)

The secret reason I don't want to get rid of our TV is the terrifying tangle of cables behind it. I'm intimidated by Scart leads; I believe, if I unplug one, it will never be possible to find the right socket again and the world will end.

Our annual Great TV Set Discussion is reaching its climax. I must go and fetch the strawberries and cream.

Completion

This week, fingers crossed, we may exchange contracts on the sale of our flat and the purchase of a house. Then we will have to agree on a date for 'completion'. What a charming word that is; like a dainty euphemism for something else entirely.

It occurs to me that the whole business is like an old-fashioned arranged marriage, conducted with stately decorum. The language is quaintly antique: we are the 'vendor' and people don't come to look round the property, they 'make an appointment to view'. Meanwhile the polite and soberly suited estate agents act as go-betweens, passing on questions and worries, and delivering replies. Etiquette demands that the vendor and the buyer should not meet face to face until after the exchange of contracts (like the bride and groom on the wedding day).

An 'offer' is made and is graciously accepted. You feel everyone should give a low bow at this stage. Then, with a fanfare of form-filling, the lawyers make their entrance into the proceedings. Their role is to add a sense of mystery. They communicate with each other, but not with you. You are like an engaged couple, having to endure vague acquaintances gossiping about you behind your back.

It's traditional for a surveyor to become involved. He

effectively plays the part of the unsuitable best man at this wedding. You pay him a substantial sum of money to produce a report telling you the whole thing is a big mistake. And who are those people tutting in the background like a pair of sour spinster aunts? They are the mortgage companies, of course, and, in their opinion, this thing will never last. They wouldn't trust the groom farther than they could throw him and the bride's no better than she ought to be. They are having a great time.

No wonder, just now, I feel like a man on his wedding day – agitated and slightly sick.

Don't Wish to Know

Scientists at Boston University have devised a genetic test to tell you, with 77 per cent accuracy, if you are going to live to be a hundred. I must say, whether I'm going to make it past ninety-nine is very near the top of my list of A Hundred Things I Do Not Wish To Know. It's way up there with knowing the precise date when the world's last glacier melts into the sea, what depressingly grisly things will occur in the last ever episode of *EastEnders*, and whether the security services have decided that the current threat of a terrorist attack is imminent or merely severe.

Here are some other things I do not wish to know: the rules of Australian football, the salary of the head of Barclays Bank, all the words of 'Winter Wonderland' and how to make the perfect blancmange.

Please do not take the trouble to inform me about where I can get the cheapest car insurance – particularly because I don't own a car. I wish to remain ignorant of the things that can go wrong with the Large Hadron Collider, the best way to skin a rabbit, and the rules of Texas hold 'em poker. And don't tell me what Peter Andre has been up to lately.

I will go to great lengths to avoid knowing the exact size of the deficit and anybody's star sign. I will stick my fingers in my ears and go la-la-la-la if you try to fill me in on the art of grouting or the miracle ingredient in shampoo which makes hair bouncy and glossy. The same goes for new improved toothpaste.

I'm determined to muddle through without finding out what zero gravity feels like or snail porridge tastes like.

There, all that took my mind off the dreary subjects of death and ageing. I recommend it as a game for all the family.

Name Overload

Do you suffer from name overload? The woman from the store telephones you and says she is called Suzanne and she's ringing about your order; the man from the gas company announces that his name is Clive; it says on the wine bar till receipt that your waitress was called Kiara. The supermarket check-out girl has her name on her lapel and the ticket inspector on the train has a little badge that introduces him as Jeff. Immediately and automatically, you forget all these names. In your brain they are filed away with all the other bits of information you will never ever need again.

I suppose it is all done in the name of transparency. Someone in the marketing department thinks that bandying about all these first names creates a nice feeling of trust. With me it does just the opposite. I bet if you addressed the ticket inspector as Jeff he wouldn't realise you were talking to him. Jeff is just his *nom de plume*, or, in this case, *nom de billet*. I bet his name is really Gervase or Dominic, but it has been decided Jeff would be more pally, more in keeping with the ethos of the company. And the check-out girl actually lost her name badge and borrowed the one belonging to her best friend who works at the delicatessen counter and is on her day off.

In fact, my theory is that none of these people are who they say they are. They are like the chap in the Bangalore call centre who insists his name is Stephen or Jake. If a girl called Jean or Mary applies for a job in the wine bar, I bet the manager tells her they prefer something a little more exotic so she will have to be known by her stage name – Ariadne or Rosa.

And perhaps Suzanne (the one from the store who phoned you earlier, remember?) does not exist at all. There is no Suzanne there; she is the one all calls are transferred to and she is always on her break or attending to another customer. Similarly, at the gas company they have a tradition going back years that everyone in the customer relations department must be called Clive. It makes things simpler when dealing with the punters.

Still, I always make a point of looking at the ticket inspector's lapel badge, in the hope that one day I will learn that his name is Anon.

Fantasy Life

Costume Drama

Here is my cut-out-and-keep recipe for Writing a Successful Television Costume Drama:

You start with Mama. The thing about Mama is that she is frequently vexed. This is because her daughter is headstrong. She is also vexed because Papa is ruined. You can tell Papa is ruined because he holds a quill pen, pores over a piece of parchment and frowns. When not vexed, Mama is most anxious. Occasionally, it all gets too much for her and she is weary. She confides in her headstrong daughter: 'It wearies me so, my child.'

You are also going to need an aunt. This aunt will wear a slightly more absurd bonnet than everyone else. She will clutch a lace hankie and signal every development of the plot by wailing. Mama should say: 'Oh, do compose yourself, Emily,' in a vexed tone of voice.

Young female characters should begin every sentence with the word 'Why'. As in 'Why, Mama, I do believe you are vexed.' Female servants do the same. So, in the (obligatory) hairbrushing scene in the heroine's bedroom, Martha will say: 'Why, Miss Elizabeth, you don't want to go filling your head with notions like that.' This is almost certainly a response to the line: 'I think, Martha, that I shall never marry. To marry would be perfectly horrid.'

Flared nostrils are essential. The heroine must ride a horse which flares its nostrils and shows the whites of its eyes. This is how we can tell that she is headstrong and spirited. At some stage, on horseback in attractive country surroundings, she must say to the leading man: 'I'll race you to that spot over there, Mr Anstruther.' There is no finishing post in this race; Miss Elizabeth stops when she is ahead and says: 'Why, Mr Anstruther, I do declare that I have won.' Not only is she spirited and headstrong, she is also a cheat. Surprisingly, Mr Anstruther is not vexed.

If the horse whinnies, it is a sign that, at some stage, Miss Elizabeth is going to be thrown off. If so, write a scene in which she lies palely on a sofa and Mr Anstruther calls upon her to find out how she is and she says: 'Why, somewhat improved, I thank you for your concern, Mr Anstruther.' Mama, meanwhile, is anxious and Aunt Emily is on her ninth lace hankie. You may prefer to make the whinnying horse trample a groom, so that Miss Elizabeth can gallop off, showing she is even more headstrong than we thought.

Young ladies doing embroidery are pure, plain and secretly in love with the man standing closest to the fireplace in the big drawing-room scene. They can never declare their feelings. Playing the harpsichord is also a bad sign. As the saying goes: 'Lucky at harpsichord, unlucky in love.'

When Miss Elizabeth tells her harpsichord-playing friend that she and Mr Anstruther are to be married, make sure that the harpsichord friend is inordinately thrilled and delighted. Being pure, plain and sad, she always rejoices in the happiness of others.

Standing by the fireplace is another bad sign. People go to the fireplace to announce bad news – e.g. 'I fear our kinsman Lord Caramel has perished in the Indies.' Papa goes to warm his backside from time to time and repeat, 'I am ruined.'

It is also the position taken up by wet young men who don't realise that the embroidering girls are in love with them. Make sure that your interesting characters lurk near the drawing-room door. Remember, however, that there are degrees of lurking. If your moody hero over-lurks he may be mistaken for the squire's embittered illegitimate son.

In the big ball scene, do not write dialogue for your leading characters while they are taking part in the sedate formation dance. It is too difficult for the actors to deliver their lines while remembering the moves of the dance. The young ladies (even the headstrong ones) look demure and the gentlemen put on intense expressions, as they think, 'Left, left together. Forward, right together.'

Finally, you will need a neatly trimmed hedge for the proposal scene when Miss Elizabeth says: 'I fear you must think me a very foolish young woman', and the hero, having abandoned lurking, replies: 'On the contrary, I have long admired you.'

Bach's Goldfish

I have been wondering lately whether Johann Sebastian Bach ever had a goldfish. He had twenty children, so the chances are one of them might have come home with one in a bag, having won it at a Weimar funfair for throwing wooden balls at plates. I suppose the great man might have thought: 'Well, at least it makes a change from all the pale pink teddy bears the other nineteen children have been winning.'

Maybe the goldfish bowl stood on top of the harpsi-chord where the great man sat and composed. Sometimes his wife would say to him, 'Never mind about that *Brandenburg Concerto*, Johann, the goldfish's water needs changing. It has gone all murky.' Bach would sigh and carry the slopping bowl to the kitchen, thinking: 'I've got twenty children; surely one of them could do this.' The goldfish always seemed lethargic as it circled the bowl, pouting languidly. It never really responded to his music. Bach wondered if all his children were taking turns to overfeed it.

These thoughts have been prompted by the report that experiments conducted at a Tokyo university suggest that goldfish can tell the difference between Bach's *Toccata and Fugue in B Minor* and Stravinsky's *Rite of Spring*. Some even have preferences, apparently.

My theory is that Bach put a huge effort into his music in a desperate attempt to get a reaction from that goldfish. Then one day, while playing a prelude from the *Well-Tempered Clavier*, he absolutely lost it, slammed the lid of the harpsichord in a fury, picked up the bowl and tipped the fish down the drain. Somehow it survived in the sewers and it bred and today its descendants still have a feeling for Bach's music.

Apart from this, there is absolutely nothing interesting to be said about goldfish and no amount of experiments in Tokyo universities, or anywhere else, can do anything to change this.

Corrections

The start of a new year is the time to take stock and, where necessary, put things right. Looking back over the past twelve months of writing in these pages, I find there were one or two occasions when I was not entirely accurate, so I am taking this opportunity to publish some corrections and clarifications.

I see now that I may have been rather carried away when compiling my list of the Ten Most Ridiculous Vegetables, so I should like to offer my apologies to members of the Courgette Appreciation Society for any hurt feelings.

Owing to a typing error, I suggested that Mr Cyril F. Whitlock, of Malmesbury, was suffering from the plague. This caused most of his friends and neighbours to shun him for the whole of June and most of July. Of course, I meant to say Mr Whitlock was suffering from plaque, a common dental condition which is not infectious. This should not be seen as a reflection on the competence of Mr Whitlock's dentist.

It was, of course, a young lady from Riga who went for a ride on a tiger. It was never my intention to suggest that the young ladies of Niger are in the habit of engaging in dangerous sports with big cats. (Anyone who has listened to a news bulletin will know that the country is pronounced 'Nee-jare' and there is no such creature as a tee-jare.)

I honestly thought that Cuthbert Watkyns-Windyridge was a made-up name. My thanks to the fourteen Cuthbert Watkyns-Windyridges who have written in to put me right.

Last March I made a jocular reference the ZB17 counter-clockwise X49 double-headed 3mm spindle shaft. This was an elementary schoolboy howler. Many readers have pointed out that I should have referred to the 2.5mm version.

Medieval Fitness

The 5:2 Diet – in which you eat normally for five days a week and hardly at all for two non-consecutive days – is not, after all, a recent fad. We are told that the same sort of regime was observed by monks in the Middle Ages. This comes as no surprise to me; I believe that our ancestors in those times were tremendous fitness freaks. You can see evidence of this in the wonderful gothic architecture of the great medieval gyms, where the monks would go to exercise and relax after hours spent producing their beautiful illuminated manuscripts, which presented their work-out programmes.

Some historians even argue that this period is known as the Middle Ages because of the great national obsession with reducing waistlines. They even suggest it was really the 'take-a-few-inches-off-your-middle ages'. An early form of pilates was practised on village greens on May Day and references to 'five a day' can be traced back to the ninth century, but at that time it meant five turnips.

King Henry I was said to have died of 'a surfeit of lampreys' and this led to a huge campaign to encourage sensible lamprey eating. Notices were nailed to church doors warning parishioners of the perils and they were all urged to observe a lamprey-free January.

The barons forced King John to put his seal on Magna Carta in 1215 and this document was designed to limit his powers and allow his people greater freedoms. There was, however, an important but little-known addendum in which the King also promised to undertake a rigorous detox programme.

One of the great poetic works of the Middle Ages was, of course, Chaucer's *Canterbury Tales*. Few people now realise that it was, in fact, an account of a group of regulars at the Tabard inn, in Southwark, agreeing to take part in a Fun Run to Canterbury, to raise awareness of scrofula.

Nanny State

Very few people seem to realise that a Nanny State actually exists. It is a remote island in the Pacific called Sensibilia. In 1817 a passenger ship on its way to Australia struck a reef and sank. Five nannies on their way to take up posts in the colonies commandeered a lifeboat and ordered the four cleanest members of the crew to row them ashore. Before they left the ship they just had time to fill a strongbox with a supply of bread crusts and bacon rind.

They landed on a small lush island. A suggestion by the crew members that they should build a crude shelter was firmly slapped down by the nannies. They spent their first weeks on the island walking briskly up and down the beach saying a bit of wind and rain never hurt anyone. They held out the palms of their hands so they could get the benefit of the sea air.

As the years passed they intermarried with the native population and formed a community which was to become the world's first nursocracy. The economy is based on the manufacture and export of extremely stiff hairbrushes.

It is said that three times in their history the Sensibilians have had to fight off invasions by neighbouring islanders who wanted to seize control of the lucrative hairbrush trade. On the first occasion they were repulsed when the people went out in their boats to meet the invaders and roared out, 'We're not at home to Mr Grumpy', and frightened them away. The story of these invasions is retold again and again in a traditional song, 'Once funny, twice silly, three times a smack.'

I was lucky enough to visit Sensibilia a couple of years ago and fell in love with the place. The people are incredibly polite and all have curly hair – which is said to be the result of eating bacon rind and cabbage stalks.

As I stepped ashore from my boat, the whole population of the island gathered to welcome me. Each one in turn gave me the traditional Sensibilian greeting, peering down my ear, while holding the lobe firmly between their thumb and forefinger, then saying, 'That will have to do.' It took some time before everyone had greeted me in this way.

After that a huge banquet was laid on in my honour with great vats of tapioca pudding, junket and mountains of fish-paste sandwiches. As the main guest, I also received the special delicacy which was an anonymous piece of gristle. They all watched me closely as I chewed it. I didn't realise it at the time, but if a guest spits the gristle into his handkerchief it means he is issuing a challenge to a fight to the death. The feast lasted five days and nights, mostly because of the Sensibilian custom that nobody leaves the table until every scrap of food is eaten up.

Religion plays an important part in life on the island. It is a mysterious religion which is based on the worship of something called The Magic Word. They believe that if you utter this word you can have all that your heart desires. The trouble is that nobody seems to know what it is. At religious ceremonies they gather and repeat the question: 'What is the Magic Word?' It seems that they are pleading for it to be revealed to them, so that all will be well.

The Supreme Governess of Sensibilia is Nanny Blenkinsop. Before I went for my audience with her, the young maidens prepared me, fashioning a vest of palm fronds sewn together because it is a rule that when you meet Nanny Blenkinsop you must have palm fronds next to the skin. They all lined up and took it in turns to tug sharply at my collar and beat me on the head with the flat of their hands to make my hair lie flat. As I made my way to the Governess's residence they smiled and waved and sang their haunting refrain, 'Now, Run Along With You.'

Nanny Blenkinsop greeted me graciously in her throne room, taking out a handkerchief and getting me to spit on it before she rubbed it hard on my forehead and face. The Senior Council of Nannies was holding a meeting to discuss the important issue of the day.

'The question is, should Michael Palin be permitted to visit our island and make one of his documentary programmes?' said Nanny Blenkinsop.

Several of the other nannies present said it was a bad idea because you never knew where he'd been. After a long debate, it was decided that one of them, Nanny Fothergill, would make some preliminary inquiries about the state of his fingernails and a message would be sent to him, telling him he could come, so long as he took that silly smile off his face.

Superstitions

We British are still very superstitious, according to a survey published last week and conducted by Dr Richard Wiseman of the University of Hertfordshire. We touch wood, cross our fingers, carry lucky charms, avoid walking under ladders, worry about smashing mirrors and feel uneasy about the number thirteen. Of those questioned, 77 per cent admitted they were superstitious.

I thought it was time to give an update on the things we are superstitious about:

- Never get your cat neutered on a Thursday.

- Carry a polystyrene worm in your pocket at all time to ward off VAT inspectors.

- It is unlucky to see one television satellite dish on its own. To cancel the bad luck, you must say: 'Top of the morning to you, Mr Murdoch. And how is Mrs Murdoch?' Then hop four times on your right foot.

- At a cash machine, never queue behind a man with an orange rucksack.

- When you see groups of people wearing baseball caps, remember it is: one for hassle, two for stress, three for sorted, five for dumped, six for a text message from a stranger and seven for a peanut allergy. This also applies to the number of mango pips on the side of your plate.

- Never kiss a girl whose jeans are more faded than yours.

- Green budgerigars are unlucky.

- If the ring-pull on your can of beans snaps it means that one of your computer files will be mysteriously deleted.

- *Rum before Coke: You'll meet a nice bloke. Coke before rum: He's in love with his mum.*

- Remember that 7479 is known as 'the Devil's PIN number'.

- In the airport departure lounge, before a long journey, spit three times on your boarding pass or you will find yourself seated on the aircraft next to a man who is an expert on diseases in tropical fish.

- Actors believe it is dreadfully bad luck to utter the name Andrew Neil anywhere in a theatre. If they need to refer to him they say 'the Scottish television presenter'.

- Never park next to a black VW Golf with a P on its licence plate.

- If you hold a croissant upside down all the luck will run out.

- Whistle in the sauna, repent in the sushi bar.

- When placing a garment in someone else's washing machine always give them a coin in payment. Otherwise the colours will run and your friendship will be destroyed.

- If the sum of the digits on your postcode is divisible by seven your chimney will get blown down.

- It's lucky if a pizza delivery bike crosses your path.

- When your debit card fails three times to swipe at the cash desk it means that a tall cousin from New Zealand is over here on holiday and will be getting in touch with you shortly.

- An itch on the palm of your right hand is a sign that your name has been entered for a Prize Draw.

- Look for the lucky four-leaved sprig of rocket in your salad.

- A squeezed avocado never ripens.

- If you hiccup in the gym it means that the Devil has put you on his mailing list.

- When a couple decide to move in together and the man provides the electric kettle, it means the woman will wear the trousers. If both the man and the woman possess an Aretha Franklin CD the relationship will not last. On their first night together the man should wear maroon socks for luck and the woman should have a new tattoo.

- Never cross on the stairs if the person coming down is carrying a tall skinny latte.

- A woman whose mobile phone ringtone is the theme tune of *The Magnificent Seven* will never give birth to sons.

- If you are bitten by a golden Labrador called Juno you will have a long and happy life and your warts will disappear.

Jane Austen

A record 32 million overseas visitors are expected to come here this year, lured partly by the 200th anniversary of the publication of *Pride and Prejudice*. As I believe Jane Austen once wrote: 'It is a truth universally acknowledged, that a tourist in possession of a good fortune must be in want of a ride on the London Eye.'

I can picture one group of such tourists, Mr and Mrs Bennet, from Austin (no relation), Texas, accompanied by their five unmarried daughters. Mrs Bennet, a rather silly woman, who is always on Twitter, is determined to marry her daughters off to eligible young British men, including, of course, Prince Harry.

On a trip north to visit Bronte country, Elizabeth Bennet has a trying encounter with Mr Fitzwilliam Darcy, a proud and haughty ticket inspector on Virgin trains. 'Miss Bennet,' he says coldly, 'I must inform you that you have boarded an incorrect train and I fear you must pay a penalty fare.' Elizabeth replies tartly: 'I declare, Mr Darcy, a journey on Virgin trains is penalty enough.' She vows to put any thought of the ticket inspector quite out of her head.

The headstrong sister Lydia, meanwhile, falls hopelessly in love with a soldier standing guard outside Buckingham Palace, buys a very expensive new bonnet with 'I heart Stratford-upon-Avon' on it, and finally elopes with a part-time Viking from the Viking Museum in York.

'Mama is vexed,' sister Jane confides to Elizabeth one night in their hotel room. 'She planned to marry Lydia to a member of the British Olympic equestrian team. Furthermore, she is much distressed by the loss of her Oyster card. Papa paid a visit to Tate Modern and has returned much perplexed.'

Later that night Elizabeth Bennet visits Boujis nightclub and is invited to entertain members on the harpsichord. As she plays, she notices the off-duty Darcy listening most earnestly and intently. Perhaps she misjudged him . . .

Citizenship Test

British Citizenship Exam. Part I. Written. All candidates must have a go. Time allowed: a fair bit.

History

1. In what year did George Stephenson invent the rocket salad?
2. When did Delia Smith defeat the Spanish paella?

3. Magna Carta established the offside rule in soccer. True or false?
4. Give the chemical formula of a) the Spirit of the Blitz b) the Dunkirk Spirit.
5. What was the year of the abolition of the death penalty for putting the milk in before the tea?
6. What offence was committed by Princess Michael of Kent which meant that she was forbidden to set foot outside that county?

Customs and Etiquette

1. State the difference between a butty and a bap.
2. In a washroom, do you yank down the roller towel *before* or *after* drying your hands? How many yanks? Give reasons.
3. Where would you expect to find a watershed?
4. What is the difference between a barber and a gents' hairdresser?
5. At the supermarket, whose responsibility is it to put the 'Next Customer Please' sign on the conveyor belt? The person in front or the person behind? Or the person who has purchased the greatest number of disposable nappies?
6. In a vet's waiting room, what animal traditionally has precedence a) an off-colour goldfish b) a

budgerigar with a sore throat c) an enraged
Pekinese?

7. Which of the following should not be allowed?
a) Wearing a dress like that at her age b) dogs on
the beach c) speed bumps d) TV repeats e) all
that gallivanting.

8. Is Sir Terence Conran famous as a) the man
who actually wrote Shakespeare's plays
b) the inventor of the Hovercraft c) the jockey
who rode Red Rum to victory in three Grand
Nationals d) the 'father' of the multiple choice
question?

9. Whose shout is it? Show workings to demonstrate how you reached your answer.

10. Are Plus Fours a) new examinations taken by
pre-primary school children b) accumulator bets
on Channel 4 Racing?

Sport

1. What is wrong with Spurs?
2. Name three afflictions suffered by soccer
referees.
3. In which sport is the term 'Aggers' used?
4. Define a) 'motivated' b) 'pressure' and c) 'his all'
(as in 'Michael gave his all').

5. Pole dancing is an Olympic event. True or false?

Culture

1. What was Inspector Morse's mother's maiden name?
2. Name two characters in *EastEnders* who are not murderers.
3. In *The Archers* is Brookfield Farm mostly arable or livestock?
4. What can the hands that do dishes be as soft as?
5. Who gives you extra?
6. Which one of the following is NOT the name of a rock group? a) Beware of the Bull b) Thank You for Not Smoking c) Stand Well Back from the Edge of the Platform d) Motorway Ends.
7. Why did the *Carry On* films stop?